100

EMERGENCY

BIBLE VERSES

Bible Translations Used:

HCSB: Scripture quotations marked HCSB, are taken from the Holman Christian Standard Bible®, Copyright © 1999, 2000, 2002, 2003, 2009 by Holman Bible Publishers. Used by permission. HCSB® is a federally registered trademark of Holman Bible Publishers.

KJV: Scripture quotations marked KJV are taken from the Holy Bible, King James Version. Public domain.

MSG: Scripture quotations marked MSG are taken from The Message. Copyright 1993, 1994, 1995, 1996, 2000, 2001, 2002 by Eugene H. Peterson. Used by permission of NavPress Publishing Group

NASB: quotations marked NASB are taken from the New American Standard Bible®, Copyright © 1960, 1962, 1963, 1968, 1971, 1972, 1973, 1975, 1977, 1995 by The Lockman Foundation Used by permission.

NCV: Scripture quotations marked NCV are taken from the New Century Version. Copyright © 1987, 1988, 1991 by Thomas Nelson, Inc. Used by permission. All rights reserved.

NIV: Scripture quotations marked NIV are taken from the Holy Bible, New International Version®, NIV®. Copyright © 1973, 1978, 1984, 2011 by Biblica, Inc.™ Used by permission of Zondervan. All rights reserved worldwide. www.zondervan.com The "NIV" and "New International Version" are trademarks registered in the United States Patent and Trademark Office by Biblica, Inc.™.

NKJV: Scripture quotations marked NKJV are taken from the New King James Version. Copyright © 1982 by Thomas Nelson, Inc. Used by permission. All rights reserved.

NLT: Scripture quotations marked NLT are taken from the Holy Bible, New Living Translation, copyright © 1996, 2004, 2007 by Tyndale House Foundation. Used by permission of Tyndale House Publishers, Inc. All rights reserved.

Cover design by Gearbox

ISBN: 978-1-68408-116-5

CONTENTS

A MESSAGE TO READERS

In an emergency, whom do you call? A family member? A friend? 911? Depending on the circumstances, these personal resources may be appropriate to meet your needs. But there's another source of strength and protection that's always available to you; that source is God.

The Christian faith, as communicated through the words of the Holy Bible, is a healing faith. It offers comfort in times of trouble; it provides courage to allay our fears; it promises hope, not hopelessness. For Christians, adversity is temporary, and failure is never final because believers know that the Lord always has the last word. Christ's followers understand that God continues to manifest His plan in good times and hard times. And they know that all things eventually work together for the good of those who trust in the Lord.

This book contains 100 Bible verses that you can use whenever Old Man Trouble arrives at your door. These verses can provide hope, courage, and energy for your daily journey. When you study these passages—when you place them permanently in your mind and in your heart—you'll discover that no challenge is too big for God, not even yours.

1

I am come that they might have life,
and that they might have it more abundantly.

JOHN 10:10 KJV

ACCEPTING GOD'S ABUNDANCE

Christ's promise still rings true: He came to this earth so that we might have life, abundant and eternal. The Son of God walked among us and endured the ultimate suffering, so that we, His children, might be blessed now and forever. We can claim His abundance by letting Him guide our steps, by letting Him establish our priorities, and by letting Him rule our hearts.

The abundance described in John 10:10 refers to spiritual health, not material wealth. And that's as it should be because spiritual health is far more important, far more meaningful, far more satisfying than the world's brand of prosperity. We mortals often confuse abundance with affluence. God does not. He knows that earthly wealth is fleeting, but spiritual wealth is not.

Today, will you claim the only kind of abundance that really matters? Will you slow yourself down long enough to ask your heavenly Father for guidance and protection? Will you claim His spiritual riches and experience His peace?

You can, and you should. God's abundance is available to all. Accept it, and be blessed.

MORE THOUGHTS ABOUT ABUNDANCE

God loves you and wants you to experience
peace and life—abundant and eternal.

BILLY GRAHAM

Jesus wants Life for us; Life with a capital L.

JOHN ELDREDGE

God is the giver, and we are the receivers. And His richest
gifts are bestowed not upon those who do the greatest things,
but upon those who accept His abundance and His grace.

HANNAH WHITALL SMITH

We honor God by asking for great things when they are a part
of His promise. We dishonor Him and cheat ourselves when
we ask for molehills where He has promised mountains.

VANCE HAVNER

Knowing that your future is absolutely assured
can free you to live abundantly today.

SARAH YOUNG

Submit to God, and you will have peace; then things will go well for you.

JOB 22:21 NLT

THE ART OF ACCEPTANCE

All of us encounter situations and circumstances that we wish we could change. But we can't. Sometimes the problems are simply too big for us to solve. Sometimes the things we regret happened long ago, and no matter how many times we replay the events over in our mind, the past remains unchanged. And sometimes we're swept up by life-altering events that we simply cannot control.

Reinhold Neibuhr penned a simple verse that has come to be known as the Serenity Prayer. It begins with a simple, yet profound, request: "God, grant me the serenity to accept the things I cannot change." Niebuhr's words are far easier to recite than they are to live by. Why? Because most of us want life to unfold in accordance with to our own wishes and timetables. But sometimes God has other plans.

If you've encountered unfortunate circumstances that are beyond your power to control, accept those circumstances. And trust God. When you do, you can be comforted in the knowledge that your Creator is good, that His love endures forever, and that He understands His plans perfectly, even when you do not.

MORE THOUGHTS ABOUT ACCEPTANCE

Christians who are strong in the faith grow as they accept whatever God allows to enter their lives.

BILLY GRAHAM

Acceptance says, "True, this is my situation at the moment. I'll look unblinkingly at the reality of it. But, I'll also open my hands to accept willingly whatever a loving Father sends."

CATHERINE MARSHALL

One of the marks of spiritual maturity is the quiet confidence that God is in control, without the need to understand why he does what he does.

CHARLES SWINDOLL

Accept each day as it comes to you. Do not waste your time and energy wishing for a different set of circumstances.

SARAH YOUNG

Loving Him means the thankful acceptance of all things that His love has appointed.

ELISABETH ELLIOT

3

Whoever believes that Jesus is the Christ is born of God, and everyone who loves Him who begot also loves him who is begotten of Him.

1 John 5:1 NKJV

GIVE HIM YOUR HEART

In an emergency, you need God, and you need His only begotten Son. Jesus came to this world in order that each of us might live abundantly and eternally. He came so that our joy might be complete here on Earth and, more importantly, in heaven. Christ loved us so much that He endured unspeakable pain on the cross so that we might be with Him throughout eternity.

How will you respond to Christ's sacrifice? Will you give Him your heart, your mind, and your soul? And will you accept the gift of eternal life, a gift that cost Him so much but can be yours for the asking? It's the most important decision you'll ever make. And if you choose wisely, it's a decision that you'll never regret.

MORE THOUGHTS ABOUT ACCEPTING CHRIST

The most profound essence of my nature
is that I am capable of receiving God.

St. Augustine

Choose Jesus Christ! Deny yourself, take up the Cross,
and follow Him—for the world must be shown. The world
must see, in us, a discernible, visible, startling difference.

Elisabeth Elliot

It's your heart that Jesus longs for: your will
to be made His own with self on the cross forever,
and Jesus alone on the throne.

Ruth Bell Graham

The amount of power you experience to live a victorious,
triumphant Christian life is directly proportional
to the freedom you give the Spirit to be Lord of your life!

Anne Graham Lotz

A man can accept what Christ has done without
knowing how it works; indeed, he certainly
won't know how it works until he's accepted it.

C. S. Lewis

4

God is our refuge and strength, a very present help in trouble.

PSALM 46:1 NKJV

GOD IS OUR REFUGE

From time to time, we all encounter adversity. Thankfully, we must never encounter it alone. God is always with us. When we are troubled, God stands ready and willing to protect us. Our responsibility, of course, is to ask Him for protection. When we call upon Him in prayer, He will answer—in His own time and in His own way.

The next time you're surprised by unfortunate circumstances, remember that God remains in His heaven and that He has promised to protect you. If you become discouraged with the direction of your day or your life, turn your thoughts and prayers to Him. He is a God of possibility, not negativity. He will guide you through your difficulties and beyond them. And then, with a renewed spirit of optimism and hope, you can thank the Giver for gifts that are simply too numerous to count.

MORE THOUGHTS ABOUT ADVERSITY

Often God has to shut a door in our face
so that he can subsequently open the door
through which he wants us to go.

CATHERINE MARSHALL

God alone can give us songs in the night.

C. H. SPURGEON

God is in control. He may not take away
trials or make detours for us,
but He strengthens us through them.

BILLY GRAHAM

Human problems are never
greater than divine solutions.

ERWIN LUTZER

Life is literally filled with
God-appointed storms. These squalls
surge across everyone's horizon.
We all need them.

CHARLES SWINDOLL

5

Everyone must be quick to hear, slow to speak, and slow to anger,
for man's anger does not accomplish God's righteousness.

JAMES 1:19-20 HCSB

BEYOND ANGER

Anger is harmful, hurtful, and dangerous to your spiritual health. Whenever your thoughts are hijacked by angry emotions, you forfeit the peace and perspective that might otherwise be yours. And to make matters worse, angry thoughts can cause you to behave in irrational, self-destructive ways.

When we've been hurt badly, we don't forget easily. When we can identify the person who hurt us, we naturally focus our ire on the perpetrator. Unless we can find the inner strength to forgive that person, we're likely to internalize the anger for years, for decades, or for a lifetime. Anger turned inward is always detrimental to our spiritual health and disruptive to our lives. And that's one reason—but not the only reason—that we should learn how to forgive other people quickly and completely. To do otherwise will result in needless anger and inner turmoil. If you allow anger to dominate your thoughts, it will sabotage your life and undermine your faith. To be safe, you must cleanse your heart of bitterness and resentment...and you must forgive. You must say yes to God, yes to mercy, yes to love, and no to anger.

MORE THOUGHTS ABOUT ANGER

Hot heads and cold hearts never solved anything.

BILLY GRAHAM

Life is too short to spend it
being angry, bored, or dull.

BARBARA JOHNSON

Frustration is not the will of God.
There is time to do anything and everything
that God wants us to do.

ELISABETH ELLIOT

Anger and bitterness—whatever the cause—
only end up hurting us. Turn that anger over to Christ.

BILLY GRAHAM

Hence it is not enough to deal with the Temper.
We must go to the source, and change the inmost nature,
and the angry humors will die away of themselves.

HENRY DRUMMOND

6

Be anxious for nothing, but in everything by prayer and supplication,
with thanksgiving, let your requests be made known to God.

PHILIPPIANS 4:6 NKJV

BEYOND ANXIETY

In an emergency, we we're tempted to worry. We're tempted to worry about big things, little things, and just about everything in between. To make matters worse, we live in a world that breeds anxiety and fosters fear. So it's not surprising that when we come face to face with tough times, we may fall prey to discouragement, doubt, or depression. But our Father in heaven has other plans.

God has promised that we may lead lives of abundance, not anxiety. In fact, His Word instructs us to "be anxious for nothing." But how can we put our fears to rest? By taking those fears to Him and leaving them there.

The very same God who created the universe has promised to protect you now and forever. So what do you have to worry about? With God on your side, the answer is, "Nothing."

MORE THOUGHTS ABOUT ANXIETY

Worry is the senseless process of cluttering up tomorrow's
opportunities with leftover problems from today.

BARBARA JOHNSON

Knowing that God is faithful really helps me
to not be captivated by worry.

JOSH MCDOWELL

Tomorrow is busy worrying about itself;
don't get tangled up in its worry-webs.

SARAH YOUNG

Pray, and let God worry.

MARTIN LUTHER

Do not worry about tomorrow.
This is not a suggestion, but a command.

SARAH YOUNG

7

Avoiding a fight is a mark of honor;
only fools insist on quarreling.

PROVERBS 20:3 NLT

AVOID NEEDLESS ARGUMENTS

Time and again, God's Word warns us against angry outbursts and needless arguments. Our arguments are Arguments are seldom won but often lost, so when we acquire the unfortunate habit of bickering, we do harm to our friends, to our families, to our coworkers, and to ourselves. And when we engage in petty squabbles, our losses usually outpace our gains.

Most arguments are a monumental waste of time and energy. And most quabbles do more for the devil than they do for God. So the next time you're tempted to engage in a silly squabble, slow down, catch your breath, and hold your tongue. When you do, you'll put a smile on God's face, and you'll send the devil packing.

MORE THOUGHTS ABOUT ARGUMENTS

Hot heads and cold hearts
never solved anything.

BILLY GRAHAM

Love makes everything lovely.
Hate concentrates itself on the one thing: hatred.

GEORGE MACDONALD

Watch your words diligently.
Words have such great power to bless
or to wound. When you speak
carelessly or negatively, you damage
others as well as yourself.

SARAH YOUNG

Never persist in trying to set people right.

HANNAH WHITALL SMITH

8

YOUR EMERGENCY VERSE ABOUT ASKING GOD FOR THE THINGS YOU NEED

Ask, and it will be given to you; seek, and you will find;
knock, and it will be opened to you. For everyone who asks receives,
and he who seeks finds, and to him who knocks it will be opened.

MATTHEW 7:7–8 NKJV

ALWAYS ASK

God invites us to ask Him for the things we need, and He promises to hear our prayers as well as our thoughts. The Lord is always available and He's always ready to help us. And He knows precisely what we need. But He still instructs us to ask.

Do you make a habit of asking God for the things you need? Hopefully so. After all, the Father most certainly has a plan for your life. And, He can do great things through you if you have the courage to ask for His guidance and His help. So be fervent in prayer and don't hesitate to ask the Creator for the tools you need to accomplish His plan for your life. Then get busy and expect the best. When you do your part, God will most certainly do His part. And great things are bound to happen.

SURVIVAL SKILL: ASKING GOD

It's important that you keep asking God to show you what
He wants you to do. If you don't ask, you won't know.

STORMIE OMARTIAN

God will help us become the people
we are meant to be, if only we will ask Him.

HANNAH WHITALL SMITH

God insists that we ask, not because He needs
to know our situation, but because
we need the spiritual discipline of asking.

CATHERINE MARSHALL

Are you serious about wanting God's guidance
to become a personal reality in your life?
The first step is to tell God that you know you
can't manage your own life; that you need His help.

CATHERINE MARSHALL

We honor God by asking for great things when they are a part
of His promise. We dishonor Him and cheat ourselves when
we ask for molehills where He has promised mountains.

VANCE HAVNER

The LORD bless you and keep you;
The LORD make His face shine upon you,
And be gracious to you.

NUMBERS 6:24–25 NKJV

KEEP COUNTING YOUR BLESSINGS

If you tried to count all your blessings, how long would it take? A very, very, long time. After all, you've been given the priceless gift of life here on earth and the promise of life eternal in heaven. And, you've been given so much more.

Billy Graham noted: "We should think of the blessings we so easily take for granted: Life itself; preservation from danger; every bit of health we enjoy; every hour of liberty; the ability to see, to hear, to speak, to think, and to imagine all this comes from the hand of God." That's sound advice for believers— followers of the One from Galilee—who have so much to be thankful for.

Your blessings, all of which are gifts from above, are indeed too numerous to count, but it never hurts to begin counting them anyway. It never hurts to say thanks to the Giver for the gifts you can count, and all the other ones too.

MORE THOUGHTS ABOUT BLESSINGS

God is the giver, and we are the receivers.
And His richest gifts are bestowed not upon
those who do the greatest things, but upon those
who accept His abundance and His grace.

HANNAH WHITALL SMITH

God has promised us abundance, peace,
and eternal life. These treasures are ours for the asking.
One of the great mysteries of life is why
so many of us wait so long to lay claim to God's gifts.

MARIE T. FREEMAN

God's gifts put men's best dreams to shame.

ELIZABETH BARRETT BROWNING

God is always trying to give good things to us,
but our hands are too full to receive them.

ST. AUGUSTINE

We do not need to beg Him to bless us;
He simply cannot help it.

HANNAH WHITALL SMITH

I the LORD do not change.

MALACHI 3:6 NIV

HE DOESN'T CHANGE

Here in the twenty-first century, change is a fact of life. The world keeps changing and so do we. The question, of course, is whether the changes that we initiate turn out to be improvements or impediments. To find the answer to that question, we must first consult a source of wisdom that does not change. That source is God.

God's Word promises that He does not change, so we can be comforted by the knowledge that our covenant with the Creator is everlasting and non-negotiable. The Lord has promised to keep His word, and that's precisely what He will do.

So the next time you experience an unexpected emergency or unwelcome changes, remember that one thing never changes: God's love for you. Then, perhaps, you'll worry less, do your best, and leave the rest up to Him.

MORE THOUGHTS ABOUT CHANGE

There is no growth without change, no change without
fear or loss and no loss without pain.

RICK WARREN

The world changes — circumstances change,
we change — but God's Word never changes.

WARREN WIERSBE

Will-power does not change men.
Time does not change men. Christ does.

HENRY DRUMMOND

Are you on the eve of change? Embrace it. Accept it.
Don't resist it. Change is not only a part of life,
change is a necessary part of God's strategy.
To use us to change the world, he alters our assignments.

MAX LUCADO

Change always starts in your mind.
The way you think determines the way you feel,
and the way you feel influences the way you act.

RICK WARREN

11

He who walks with integrity walks securely,
But he who perverts his ways will become known.

PROVERBS 10:9 NKJV

CHARACTER COUNTS

When times are tough, character counts. God's Word makes it clear that integrity matters to Him, so it must matter to us. If we wish to walk in the light of God's truth, we must be truthful. Honesty enriches relationships; deception destroys them.

Henry Blackaby observed, "God is interested in developing your character. At times He lets you proceed, but He will never let you go too far without discipline to bring you back." The implication is clear: Personal integrity is important to God, so it must be important to us.

Living a life of integrity isn't the easiest way, but it's always the best way. So if you find yourself tempted to break the truth—or to bend it—remember that honesty is, indeed, the best policy; it's also God's policy, so it must be your policy too.

SURVIVAL SKILLS:
CHARACTER AND INTEGRITY

The single most important element
in any human relationship is honesty—
with oneself, with God, and with others.

CATHERINE MARSHALL

Integrity is the glue that holds our way of life together.

BILLY GRAHAM

The commandment of absolute truthfulness
is only another name for the fullness of discipleship.

DIETRICH BONHOEFFER

True greatness is not measured by
the headlines or wealth. The inner character
of a person is the true measure of lasting greatness.

BILLY GRAHAM

Let your words be the genuine picture of your heart.

JOHN WESLEY

12

A merry heart does good, like medicine.

PROVERBS 17:22 NKJV

BE CHEERFUL

When tough times arrive, you may need cheering up. And if you're a Christian, you have many reasons to be cheerful: God is in His heaven; He remains firmly in control; He loves you; and through His Son, He has offered you a path to eternal life.

All of us have so much to be thankful for, but in times of adversity or pain, we may forget to count our blessings. And all of us will occasionally fall victim to the inevitable frustrations of everyday life. When stresses threaten to overwhelm us, we should pause, take a deep breath, and remember God's incalculable blessings.

Cheerfulness is a gift that we give to others and to ourselves. The joy we give to others is reciprocal: Whatever we give away is returned to us, oftentimes in greater measure. So make this promise to yourself and keep it: Be a cheerful ambassador for Christ. He deserves no less, and neither, for that matter, do you.

SURVIVAL SKILL: CHEERFULNESS

A life of intimacy with God is characterized by joy.

OSWALD CHAMBERS

It is not fitting, when one is in God's service,
to have a gloomy face or a chilling look.

ST. FRANCIS OF ASSISI

The practical effect of Christianity is happiness,
therefore let it be spread abroad everywhere!

C. H. SPURGEON

The greatest honor you can give Almighty God is to live
gladly and joyfully because of the knowledge of His love.

JULIANA OF NORWICH

God is good, and heaven is forever. And if those
two facts don't cheer you up, nothing will.

MARIE T. FREEMAN

13

I am offering you life or death, blessings or curses. Now, choose life!…
To choose life is to love the LORD your God, obey him, and stay close to him.

DEUTERONOMY 30:19-20 NCV

CHOOSE WISELY

Your life is a series of choices, and those choices matter because the quality of your choices has a direct impact on the quality and direction of your life. When you choose wisely, you'll be blessed by a heavenly Father who rewards believers who honor Him and follow in the footsteps of His Son.

As Christians who have been saved by a loving and merciful God, we have every reason to make wise choices. Yet sometimes, when caught up in the hustle and bustle of life here on earth, we may behave in ways that are displeasing to our Creator. When we do, we forfeit—albeit temporarily—the peace and abundance that we might otherwise experience through Him.

Today, take time to consider how many things in this life you can control: your thoughts, your words, your actions, and your priorities, for starters. Then make choices that are pleasing to the Lord.

MORE THOUGHTS ABOUT CHOICES

Your little choices become habits that affect
the bigger decisions you make in life.

ELIZABETH GEORGE

Every choice you make has an end result.

ZIG ZIGLAR

There are two great forces at work
in the world today: the unlimited power of God
and the limited power of Satan.

CORRIE TEN BOOM

God always gives His very best to those
who leave the choice with Him.

HUDSON TAYLOR

We first make our habits, then our habits make us.

JOHN DRYDEN

14

As the Father loved Me, I also have loved you; abide in My love.

JOHN 15:9 NKJV

HIS LOVE CHANGES EVERYTHING

Jesus loves us so much that He willingly sacrificed Himself on the cross so that we might live with Him throughout eternity. His love endures. Even when we falter, He loves us. When we fall prey to the world's temptations, He remains steadfast. In fact, no power on Earth can separate us from His love.

Christ's love can transform us. When we open our hearts to Him and walk in His footsteps, our lives bear testimony to His mercy and to His grace. Yes, Christ's love changes everything. May we welcome Him into our hearts so that He can then change everything in us.

SURVIVAL SKILL: CHRIST'S LOVE

Jesus is all compassion.
He never betrays us.

CATHERINE MARSHALL

Above all else, the Christian life
is a love affair of the heart.

JOHN ELDREDGE

Jesus: the proof of God's love.

PHILLIP YANCEY

As the love of a husband for his bride,
such is the love of Christ for His people.

C. H. SPURGEON

The love of God exists in its strongest
and purest form in the very midst
of suffering and tragedy.

SUZANNE DALE EZELL

15

I have learned to be content in whatever circumstances I am.

PHILIPPIANS 4:11 HCSB

OVERCOMING DIFFICULT CIRCUMSTANCES

All of us must endure difficult circumstances, those tough times when our faith is tested and our strength is stretched to the limit. We find ourselves in situations that we didn't ask for and probably don't deserve. During these difficult days, we try our best to "hold up under the circumstances." But God has a better plan. He intends for us to rise above our circumstances, and He's promised to help us do it.

Are you dealing with a difficult situation or a tough problem? Do you struggle with occasional periods of discouragement and doubt? Are you worried, weary, or downcast? If so, don't face tough times alone. Face them with God as your partner, your protector, and your guide. Talk to Him often, ask for His guidance, and listen carefully for His response. When you do, He will give you the strength to meet any challenge, the courage to face any problem, and the patience to endure—and to eventually rise above— any circumstance.

MORE THOUGHTS ABOUT CIRCUMSTANCES

We all go through pain and sorrow, but the presence of God,
like a warm, comforting blanket, can shield us and protect
us, and allow the deep inner joy to surface, even in the most
devastating circumstances.

BARBARA JOHNSON

In all the old castles of England, there was a place called the
keep. It was always the strongest and best protected place
in the castle, and in it were hidden all who were weak and
helpless and unable to defend themselves in times of danger.
Shall we be afraid to hide ourselves in the keeping power of
our Divine Keeper, who neither slumbers nor sleeps, and
who has promised to preserve our going out and our coming
in, from this time forth and even forever more?

HANNAH WHITALL SMITH

God has a purpose behind every problem.
He uses circumstances to develop our character.
In fact, he depends more on circumstances to make us
like Jesus than he depends on our reading the Bible.

RICK WARREN

When you fall and skin your knees
and skin your heart, He'll pick you up.

CHARLES STANLEY

16

Do everything without complaining or arguing.
Then you will be innocent and without any wrong.

PHILIPPIANS 2:14–15 NCV

NO COMPLAINTS

Most of us have more blessings than we can count, yet we still find things to complain about. To complain, of course, is not only shortsighted, but it is also a serious roadblock on the path to spiritual abundance. But in our weakest moments we still grumble, whine, and moan. Sometimes we give voice to our complaints, and on other occasions, we manage to keep our protestations to ourselves. But even when no one else hears our complaints, God does.

Would you like to feel more comfortable about your circumstances and your life? Then promise yourself that you'll do whatever it takes to ensure that you focus your thoughts and energy on the major blessings you've received, not the minor hardships you must occasionally endure.

So the next time you're tempted to complain about the inevitable frustrations of everyday living, don't do it. Today and every day, make it a practice to count your blessings, not your inconveniences. It's the truly decent way to live.

MORE THOUGHTS ABOUT COMPLAINING

Thanksgiving or complaining—these words express
two contrasting attitudes of the souls of God's children.
The soul that gives thanks can find comfort in everything;
the soul that complains can find comfort in nothing.

HANNAH WHITALL SMITH

If we have our eyes upon ourselves, our problems,
and our pain, we cannot lift our eyes upward.

BILLY GRAHAM

It is always possible to be thankful for what is given
rather than to complain about what is not given.
One or the other becomes a habit of life.

ELISABETH ELLIOT

Don't complain. The more you complain about things,
the more things you'll have to complain about.

E. STANLEY JONES

Grumbling and gratitude are, for the child of God,
in conflict. Be grateful and you won't grumble.
Grumble and you won't be grateful.

BILLY GRAHAM

17

*So we may boldly say: "The L*ORD *is my helper;*
I will not fear. What can man do to me?"

HEBREWS 13:6 NKJV

BE CONFIDENT

As Christians, we have every reason live confidently. After all, we've read God's promises and we know that He's prepared a place for us in heaven. And with God on our side, what should we fear? The answer, of course, is, "Nothing." But sometimes, despite our faith and despite God's promises, we find ourselves gripped by earthly apprehensions.

When we focus on our doubts and fears, we can concoct a lengthy list of reasons to lie awake at night and fret about the uncertainties of the coming day. A better strategy, of course, is to focus, not upon our fears, but instead upon our God.

In an emergency, you need confidence, and if you're a Christian, you should be extremely confident. After all, God's promises never fail and His love is everlasting. So the next time you need a boost of confidence, slow down and have a little chat with your Creator. Count your blessings, not your troubles. Focus on possibilities, not problems. And remember that with God on your side, you have absolutely nothing to fear.

SURVIVAL SKILL: CONFIDENCE

You need to make the right decision—
firmly and decisively—
and then stick with it, with God's help.

BILLY GRAHAM

We need to recognize that lack of confidence
does not equal humility. In fact,
genuinely humble people have enormous
confidence because it rests in a great God.

BETH MOORE

Never yield to gloomy anticipation.

LETTIE COWMAN

Confidence in the natural world is self-reliance;
in the spiritual world, it is God-reliance.

OSWALD CHAMBERS

We never get anywhere—nor do our conditions
and circumstances change—
when we look at the dark side of life.

LETTIE COWMAN

*Jesus replied, "I assure you: Unless someone is born again,
he cannot see the kingdom of God."
"But how can anyone be born when he is old?"
Nicodemus asked Him. "Can he enter his mother's womb
a second time and be born?"
Jesus answered, "I assure you: Unless someone is born of water
and the Spirit, he cannot enter the kingdom of God."*

JOHN 3:3–5 HCSB

BORN AGAIN

The Son of God walked among us. He lived, loved, preached, healed, taught, and died on the cross. He did it for us. And He wants us to join Him forever in heaven.

Ours is not a distant God. He is always present, always ready to guide and protect us. He watches over His creation and He understands—far better than we ever could—the essence of what it means to be human.

God understands our fears, our hopes, and our temptations. He understands what it means to be angry and what it costs to forgive. He knows the heart and the conscience of every person who has ever lived, including you. And God has a plan of salvation that is intended for you. Accept it. Accept God's gift through the person of His Son and then rest assured: God walked among us so that you might have eternal life; amazing though it may seem, He did it for you.

MORE THOUGHTS ABOUT CONVERSION

Conversion is a complete surrender to Jesus.
It's a willingness to do what he wants you to do.

BILLY SUNDAY

The most important decisions you'll ever make
is the decision you make about eternity.

BILLY GRAHAM

In order to get to heaven, Jesus said that you
must be converted. I didn't say it—Jesus said it!

BILLY GRAHAM

I have never known a man who
received Christ and regretted it.

BILLY GRAHAM

The conversion of a soul is the miracle of a moment,
but the manufacture of a saint is the task of a lifetime.

ALAN REDPATH

19

Be strong and courageous, and do the work.
Do not be afraid or discouraged, for the Lord God, my God, is with you.

1 Chronicles 28:20 NIV

COURAGE FOR TODAY

As believers in a risen Christ, we can, and should, live courageously. After all, Jesus promises us that He has overcome the world and that He has made a place for us in heaven. So we have nothing to fear in the long term because our Lord will care for us throughout eternity. But what about those short-term, everyday worries that keep us up at night? And what about the life-altering hardships that leave us wondering if we can ever recover? The answer, of course, is that because God cares for us in good times and hard times, we can turn our concerns over to Him in prayer, knowing that all things ultimately work for the good of those who love Him.

When you form a one-on-one relationship with your Creator, you can be comforted by the fact that wherever you find yourself, whether at the top of the mountain or the depths of the valley, God is there with you. And because your Creator cares for you and protects you, you can rise above your fears.

At this very moment the Lord is seeking to work in you and through you. He's asking you to live abundantly and courageously, and He's ready to help. So why not let Him do it...starting now?

SURVIVAL SKILL: COURAGE

Courage is not simply one of the virtues,
but the form of every virtue at the testing point.

C. S. LEWIS

Action springs not from thought,
but from a readiness for responsibility.

DIETRICH BONHOEFFER

Just as courage is faith in good, so discouragement is
faith in evil, and, while courage opens the door to good,
discouragement opens it to evil.

HANNAH WHITALL SMITH

In my experience, God rarely makes our fear disappear.
Instead, he asks us to be strong and take courage.

BRUCE WILKINSON

Do not limit the limitless God! With Him, face the future
unafraid because you are never alone.

LETTIE COWMAN

20

He will not fear bad news; his heart is confident,
trusting in the Lord. His heart is assured; he will not fear.

PSALM 112:7-8 HCSB

IN EVERY CRISIS, SAY YES TO GOD

Your decision to seek a deeper relationship with Christ will not remove all problems from your life; to the contrary, it will bring about a series of personal crises as you constantly seek to say yes to God although the world encourages you to do otherwise. You live in a world that seeks to snare your attention and lead you away from the Lord. Each time you are tempted to distance yourself from your Creator, you'll face a spiritual crisis. A few of these crises may be monumental in scope, but most will be the small, seemingly inconsequential decisions of everyday life. In fact, life here on earth can be seen as one test after another—and with each crisis comes yet another opportunity to grow closer to the Lord or to distance yourself from Him.

Today, you will face many opportunities to say yes to your Creator—and you will also encounter many opportunities to say no. Your answers will determine the quality of your day and the direction of your life, so please answer carefully.

MORE THOUGHTS ABOUT CRISIS

God will make obstacles serve His purpose.

LETTIE COWMAN

When a train goes through a tunnel and it gets dark,
you don't throw away your ticket and jump off.
You sit still and trust the engineer.

CORRIE TEN BOOM

No faith is so precious as that which triumphs over adversity.

C. H. SPURGEON

The sermon of your life in tough times ministers to people
more powerfully than the most eloquent speaker.

BILL BRIGHT

The great thing with unhappy times is to take them bit by bit,
hour by hour, like an illness. It is seldom the present,
the exact present, that is unbearable.

C. S. LEWIS

21

Don't be deceived: God is not mocked. For whatever a man sows he will also reap, because the one who sows to his flesh will reap corruption from the flesh, but the one who sows to the Spirit will reap eternal life from the Spirit.

GALATIANS 6:7-8 HCSB

WISE DECISIONS

Each day you must make countless decisions. Many of those decisions are so tightly woven into the fabric of your life that you scarcely realize that they are decisions at all. Other decisions are made purely out of habit. But occasionally, you'll find yourself at one of life's inevitable crossroads, and when you do, it's time to slow down and have a heart-to-heart talk with the ultimate Counselor: your Father in heaven.

The Bible offers clear guidance about decision making. So if you're about to make an important decision, here are some things you can do: 1. Gather information. Don't expect to get all the facts—that's impossible—but try to gather as much information as you can in a reasonable amount of time (Proverbs 24:3-4). 2. Be patient: If you have time to make a decision, use that time to make a good decision (Proverbs 19:2). 3. Rely on the counsel of a few friends and mentors. Proverbs 1:5 makes it clear: "A wise man will hear and increase learning, and a man of understanding will attain wise counsel." (NKJV). 4. Pray for guidance and listen carefully to your conscience. "Guide me in your truth and teach me, for you are God my Savior, and my hope is in you all day long." (Psalm 25:5). 5. When the time for action arrives, act. Procrastination is the enemy of progress; don't let it defeat you (James 1:22).

MORE THOUGHTS ABOUT DECISIONS

A man who honors God privately will show it
by making good decisions publically.

EDWIN LOUIS COLE

Every day, I find countless opportunities to decide
whether I will obey God and demonstrate my love
for Him or try to please myself or the world system.
God is waiting for my choices.

BILL BRIGHT

Get into the habit of dealing with God about everything.

OSWALD CHAMBERS

Your choices and decisions are a reflection of how well
you've set and followed your priorities.

ELIZABETH GEORGE

22

Bad temper is contagious—don't get infected.

PROVERBS 22:25 MSG

DEALING WITH DIFFICULT PEOPLE

Unless you lead a solitary life, living alone and never leaving your own home, you'll encounter difficult people. Lots of difficult people. Why? Because they're everywhere: in all walks of life, in all economic strata, in every profession, and in ever large institution.

So what should we do about the difficult people who inhabit our lives and invade our psyches? First, we should realize that God sometimes uses difficult people to achieve His plans for our lives. These people have much to teach us about ourselves, so we should examine every encounter to determine if God is using our adversaries to advance our own spiritual growth.

In addition to teaching us valuable lessons about life, difficult people also teach us about spiritual virtues such as patience, perseverance, forgiveness, and courage. Oftentimes, our antagonists teach us lessons we could learn in no other way. So, instead of fretting about the prickly personalities who inhabit your life, open your heart to God's guidance and His love. Listen to Him, and treat all His children with love and respect. When you do, you'll be a blessing to all those whom God has seen fit to place along your path.

MORE THOUGHTS ABOUT DEALING WITH DIFFICULT PEOPLE

We are all fallen creatures and all very hard to live with.

C. S. LEWIS

We must meet our disappointments, our malicious enemies, our provoking friends, our trials of every sort, with an attitude of surrender and trust. We must rise above them in Christ so they lose their power to harm us.

HANNAH WHITALL SMITH

If you are a Christian, you are not a citizen of this world trying to get to heaven; you are a citizen of heaven making your way through this world.

VANCE HAVNER

Give me such love for God and men as will blot out all hatred and bitterness.

DIETRICH BONHOEFFER

23

Jesus said, "Don't let your hearts be troubled.
Trust in God, and trust in me."

JOHN 14:1 NCV

DEALING WITH DISAPPOINTMENTS

As we make the journey from the cradle to the grave, disappointments are inevitable. No matter how competent we are, no matter how fortunate, we still encounter circumstances that fall far short of our expectations. When tough times arrive, we have choices to make: We can feel sorry for ourselves, or we can get angry, or we can become depressed. Or we can get busy praying about out problems and solving them.

When we are disheartened—on those cloudy days when our strength is sapped and our hope is shaken—there exists a source from which we can draw perspective and courage. That source is God. When we turn everything over to Him, we find that He is sufficient to meet our needs. No problem is too big for Him.

So the next time you feel discouraged, slow down long enough to have a serious talk with your Creator. Pray for guidance, pray for strength, and pray for the wisdom to trust your heavenly Father. Your troubles are temporary; His love is not.

MORE THOUGHTS
ABOUT DISAPPOINTMENTS

We all have sorrows and disappointments,
but one must never forget that, if commended to God,
they will issue in good. His own solution
is far better than any we could conceive.

FANNY CROSBY

Let God enlarge you when you are
going through distress. He can do it.

WARREN WIERSBE

Unless we learn to deal with disappointment,
it will rob us of joy and poison our souls.

BILLY GRAHAM

If your hopes are being disappointed just now,
it means that they are being purified.

OSWALD CHAMBERS

Discouragement is the opposite of faith.
It is Satan's device to thwart the work of God in your life.

BILLY GRAHAM

"Follow Me," Jesus told them, "and I will make you make you fish for people!" Immediately they left their nets and followed Him.

MARK 1:17-18 HCSB

DISCIPLESHIP NOW

Jesus instructed His disciples to "take up his cross" and follow Him. His disciples must have known exactly what the Master meant. In Christ's day, prisoners were forced to carry their own crosses to the location where they would be put to death. So the message was clear: In order to follow Him, the disciples must deny themselves and, instead, trust Him completely. Nothing has changed since then.

If we are to be disciples of Christ, we must put Him first in our thoughts and our lives. Jesus never comes next. He is always first. The paradox, of course, is that only by sacrificing ourselves to Him do we gain salvation for ourselves.

Do you want to be a worthy disciple of Christ? Then pick up your cross today, tomorrow, and every day that you live. When you do, He will bless you today, tomorrow, and forever.

SURVIVAL SKILL: DISCIPLESHIP

Our Lord's conception of discipleship is not that we work for
God, but that God works through us.

OSWALD CHAMBERS

His voice leads us not into timid
discipleship but into bold witness.

CHARLES STANLEY

Discipleship usually brings us into the necessity
of choice between duty and desire.

ELISABETH ELLIOT

Jesus challenges you and me to keep our focus daily
on the cross of His will if we want to be His disciples.

ANNE GRAHAM LOTZ

To be a disciple of Jesus means to learn from Him,
to follow Him. The cost may be high.

BILLY GRAHAM

25

Immediately the father of the child cried out and said with tears,
"Lord, I believe; help my unbelief!"

Mark 9:24 NKJV

BEYOND THE DOUBTS

When tough times arrive, we're tempted to abandon hope. That's when fears and doubts have a way of hijacking our thoughts and derailing our plans. Even the most faithful Christians are overcome by occasional bouts of fear and doubt. You are no different.

When your faith is being tested to its limits, seek the comfort and assurance of the One who sent His Son as a sacrifice for you.

Have you ever felt your trust in God slipping away? Have you begun to doubt yourself, your faith, or your future? If so, you are not alone. Every life—including yours—is a series of successes and failures, joys and sorrows, celebrations and disappointments, hopes and doubts.

When times are good, it's easy to praise God and thank Him for His blessings. But when hard times arrive, as they inevitably will, it's harder to be grateful. Harder but not impossible. Even when you feel very distant from God, God is never distant from you. When you sincerely seek His presence, He will touch your heart, calm your fears, and restore your soul.

MORE THOUGHTS ABOUT DOUBTS

Doubt is not always a sign that a man is wrong;
it may be a sign that he is thinking.

OSWALD CHAMBERS

Have you been tormented with fears and doubts?
Bombarded with temptation to sin?
Try praising the Lord, and watch Satan flee.

NANCY LEIGH DEMOSS

We are most vulnerable to the piercing winds
of doubt when we distance ourselves from the mission
and fellowship to which Christ has called us.

JONI EARECKSON TADA

Fear and doubt are conquered by a faith that rejoices.
And faith can rejoice because the promises
of God are as certain as God Himself.

KAY ARTHUR

Doubt is not the opposite of faith; it is one element of faith.

PAUL TILLICH

*Now may the God of hope fill you with all joy and peace as you believe
in Him so that you may overflow with hope by the power of the Holy Spirit.*

ROMANS 15:13 HCSB

YOUR BIG DREAMS

Do you consider the future to be friend or foe? Do you expect the best, and are you willing to work for it? If so, please consider the fact that the Lord expects each of us to do the hard work required to achieve our dreams. And He's especially helpful to those of us who consult Him before we finalize our plans.

God's help is always available to those ask. Our job, of course, is to seek His guidance and His strength as we seek to accomplish His plans for our lives.

Nothing is too difficult for God, and no dreams are too big for Him—not even yours. When you do your part, He'll do His part, and great things are bound to happen. So live confidently, plan carefully, do your best, and leave the rest up to the Creator. You and He, working together, can move mountains. Lots of them.

MORE THOUGHTS ABOUT DREAMS

Allow your dreams a place in your prayers and plans.
God-given dreams can help you move
into the future He is preparing for you.

BARBARA JOHNSON

Perhaps the greatest psychological, spiritual, and medical
need that all people have is the need for hope.

BILLY GRAHAM

When the dream of our heart is one that God has planted
there, a strange happiness flows into us. At that moment,
the spiritual resources of the universe are released to help us.

CATHERINE MARSHALL

God's gifts put men's best dreams to shame.

ELIZABETH BARRETT BROWNING

Two types of voices command your attention today.
Negative ones fill your mind with doubt, bitterness,
and fear. Positive ones purvey hope and strength.
Which one will you choose to heed?

MAX LUCADO

But encourage each other daily, while it is still called today,
so that none of you is hardened by sin's deception.

HEBREWS 3:13 HCSB

THE POWER OF ENCOURAGEMENT

Whether we realize it or not, all of us need encouragement. The world can be a difficult place, a place where we encounter the inevitable disappointments that are woven into the fabric of everyday life. So we all need boosters who are ready, willing, and able to cheer us on when times get tough.

God's Word teaches that we must treat others as we ourselves wish to be treated. Since we desire encouragement for ourselves, we should be quick to share it with others.

Whom will you encourage today? How many times will you share a smile, or a kind word, or a pat on the back? You'll probably have many opportunities to share the gift of encouragement. When you seize those opportunities, others will be blessed, and you'll be blessed too. But not necessarily in that order.

SURVIVAL SKILL: ENCOURAGEMENT

Discouraged people don't need critics. They hurt
enough already. What they need is encouragement.
They need a refuge, a willing, caring, available someone.

CHARLES SWINDOLL

All around you are people whose lives
are filled with trouble and sorrow.
They need your compassion and encouragement.

BILLY GRAHAM

Developing a positive attitude means working continually
to find what is uplifting and encouraging.

BARBARA JOHNSON

Don't forget that a single sentence, spoken at the right
moment, can change somebody's whole perspective on life. A
little encouragement can go a long, long way.

MARIE T. FREEMAN

When we are the comfort and encouragement
to others, we are sometimes surprised
at how it comes back to us many times over.

BILLY GRAHAM

28

*Be of good courage, and he shall strengthen your heart,
all ye that hope in the LORD.*

PSALM 31:24 KJV

ENERGY FOR TODAY

All of us suffer through emergencies, adversities, tough times, and difficult days. So all of us have moments when our spiritual and emotional batteries are depleted. When we feel exhausted, there's a place we can turn for comfort and strength. That source is God.

If you're a person with too many demands and too few hours in which to meet them, it's probably time to examine your priorities, and it's probably time to remove a few entries from your daily to-do list. While you're at it, ask the Lord for the wisdom to prioritize your life and the strength to fulfill your responsibilities. He will give you the energy to do the most important things on your list if you ask Him. So ask, listen, and learn...today.

MORE THOUGHTS ABOUT ENERGY

God does not dispense strength and encouragement
like a druggist fills your prescription. The Lord
doesn't promise to give us something to take
so we can handle our weary moments.
He promises us Himself. That is all. And that is enough.

CHARLES SWINDOLL

When the dream of our heart is one that God
has planted there, a strange happiness flows into us.
At that moment, all of the spiritual resources
of the universe are released to help us. Our praying
is then at one with the will of God and becomes a channel
for the Creator's purposes for us and our world.

CATHERINE MARSHALL

When we reach the end of our strength,
wisdom, and personal resources, we enter into
the beginning of his glorious provisions.

PATSY CLAIRMONT

One reason so much American Christianity is a mile
wide and an inch deep is that Christians are simply tired.
Sometimes you need to kick back and rest for Jesus' sake.

DENNIS SWANBERG

29

Whatever you do, do it enthusiastically,
as something done for the Lord and not for men.

COLOSSIANS 3:23 HCSB

YOU HAVE SO MUCH TO CELEBRATE!

As a Christian, you have many reasons to be enthusiastic about your life, your opportunities, and your future. After all, your eternal destiny is secure. Christ died for your sins, and He wants you to experience life abundant and life eternal. So what's not to get excited about?

Are you a passionate person and an enthusiastic Christian? Are you genuinely excited about your faith, your family, and your future? Hopefully, you can answer these questions with a resounding yes. But if your passion for life has waned, it's time to slow down long enough to recharge your spiritual batteries and reorder your priorities.

Each new day is an opportunity to put God first and celebrate His creation. Today, take time to count your blessings and take stock of your opportunities. And while you're at it, ask God for strength. When you sincerely petition Him, He will give you everything you need to live enthusiastically and abundantly.

SURVIVAL SKILL: ENTHUSIASM

Wherever you are, be all there.
Live to the hilt every situation
you believe to be the will of God.

JIM ELLIOT

Developing a positive attitude
means working continually to find
what is uplifting and encouraging.

BARBARA JOHNSON

Those who have achieved excellence
in the practice of an art or profession
have commonly been motivated
by great enthusiasm in their pursuit of it.

JOHN KNOX

Instead of living a black-and-white existence,
we'll be released into a Technicolor world
of vibrancy and emotion when we more accurately
reflect His nature to the world around us.

BILL HYBELS

30

Your Emergency Verse About Envy For where envy and selfish ambition exist, there is disorder and every kind of evil.

JAMES 3:16 HCSB

BEYOND ENVY

God's Word warns us about a dangerous, destructive state of mind: envy. Envy is emotional poison. It poisons the mind and hardens the heart.

If we are to experience the abundant lives that Christ has promised, we must be on guard against the envious thoughts. Jealousy breeds discontent, discontent breeds unhappiness, and unhappiness robs us of the peace that might otherwise be ours. So if the sin of envy has invaded your heart, ask God to help you heal. When you ask sincerely and often, He will respond. And when He does, you'll regain the peace that can only be found through Him.

MORE THOUGHTS ABOUT ENVY

Envy takes the joy, happiness,
and contentment out of living.

BILLY GRAHAM

How can you feel the miseries
of envy when you possess in Christ
the best of all portions?

C. H. SPURGEON

Envy shoots at others and wounds herself.

THOMAS FULLER

Envy and greed always—always—
exact a terrible price.

BILLY GRAHAM

Resentment always hurts you more
than the person you resent.

RICK WARREN

31

For God so loved the world, that he gave his only begotten Son,
that whosoever believeth in him should not perish, but have everlasting life.

JOHN 3:16 KJV

THE GIFT OF ETERNAL LIFE

Jesus is not only the light of the world; He is also its salvation. He came to this earth so that we might not perish, but instead spend eternity with Him. What a glorious gift; what a priceless opportunity.

As mere mortals, we cannot fully understand the scope, and thus the value, of eternal life. Our vision is limited but God's is not. He sees all things; He knows all things; and His plans for you extend throughout eternity.

If you haven't already done so, this moment is the perfect moment to turn your life over to God's only begotten son. When you give your heart to the Son, you belong to the Father—today, tomorrow, and for all eternity.

MORE THOUGHTS ABOUT ETERNAL LIFE

Death is not the end of life;
it is only the gateway to eternity.

BILLY GRAHAM

At most, you will live a hundred years on earth,
but you will spend forever in eternity.

RICK WARREN

Death is not a journeying into an unknown land.
It is a voyage home. We are not going to a strange country
but to our Father's house, and among our kith and kin.

JOHN RUSKIN

Everything that is joined to the immortal Head
will share His immortality.

C. S. LEWIS

You need to think more about eternity and not less.

RICK WARREN

32

For a righteous man may fall seven times and rise again.

PROVERBS 24:16 NKJV

BEYOND FAILURE

Occasional mistakes, setbacks, disappointments, and failures are the price that we must pay for taking risks and trying new things. Even the best-intentioned plans sometimes go astray, and when they do, we must never lose faith. When we fail, we must not label ourselves as "failures." Instead, we should pick ourselves up, dust ourselves off, learn from our mistakes, and reengage with life.

Have you encountered a recent setback? If so, what did you learn? And how can you apply your hard-earned wisdom to the challenges that are ahead of you?

If you've experienced a recent disappointment, remember that God still has big plans for your life. And while you're waiting for those plans to unfold, keep working, keep praying, and keep the faith. The Lord can build a road through any wilderness. Even yours.

MORE THOUGHTS ABOUT FAILURE

No matter how badly we have failed, we can always get up
and begin again. Our God is the God of new beginnings.

WARREN WIERSBE

Mistakes offer the possibility for redemption
and a new start in God's kingdom. No matter what
you're guilty of, God can restore your innocence.

BARBARA JOHNSON

Failure is one of life's most powerful teachers.
How we handle our failures determines whether
we're going to simply "get by" in life or "press on."

BETH MOORE

No amount of falls will really undo us
if we keep picking ourselves up after each one.

C. S. LEWIS

Those who have failed miserably are often
the first to see God's formula for success.

ERWIN LUTZER

33

*For I assure you: If you have faith the size of a mustard seed,
you will tell this mountain, "Move from here to there,"
and it will move. Nothing will be impossible for you.*

MATTHEW 17:20 HCSB

MOUNTAIN-MOVING FAITH

The Bible makes it clear: Faith is powerful. With it, we can move mountains. With it, we can endure any hardship. With it, we can rise above the challenges of everyday life and live victoriously, whatever our circumstances.

Is your faith strong enough to move the mountains in your own life? If so, you're already tapped in to a source of strength that never fails: God's strength. But if your spiritual batteries are in need of recharging, don't be discouraged. God's strength is always available to those who seek it.

The first element of a successful life is faith—faith in God, faith in His promises, and faith in His Son. When our faith in the Creator is strong, we can then have faith in ourselves, knowing that we are tools in the hands of a loving God who made mountains—and moves them—according to a perfect plan that only He can see.

SURVIVAL SKILL: FAITH

Shout the shout of faith. Nothing can withstand
the triumphant faith that links itself to omnipotence.
The secret of all successful living lies in this shout of faith.

HANNAH WHITALL SMITH

I have learned that faith means trusting in advance
what will only make sense in reverse.

PHILLIP YANCEY

Faith does not concern itself with the entire journey.
One step is enough.

LETTIE COWMAN

Faith is not merely holding on to God.
It is God holding on to you.

CORRIE TEN BOOM

Faith points us beyond our problems
to the hope we have in Christ.

BILLY GRAHAM

I sought the LORD, and He heard me, and delivered me from all my fears.

PSALM 34:4 NKJV

ABOVE AND BEYOND FEAR

From time to time, all of us experience emergencies that test our mettle. When these situations occur, fear creeps in and threatens to overtake our minds and our hearts.

Difficult times call for courageous measures. Running away from problems only perpetuates them. Fear begets more fear; and, anxiety is a poor counselor.

Adversity visits everyone—no human being is beyond Old Man Trouble's reach. But, Old Man Trouble is not only an unwelcome guest, he is also an invaluable teacher. If we are to become mature human beings, it is our duty to learn from the inevitable hardships and heartbreaks of life.

Today, ask God to help you step beyond the boundaries of your fear. Ask Him to guide you to a place where you can realize your potential—a place where you are freed from the paralysis of anxiety. Ask Him to do His part, and then promise Him that you'll do your part. Don't ask God to lead you to a safe place; ask Him to lead you to the right place. And remember that those two places are seldom the same.

MORE THOUGHTS ABOUT FEAR

The presence of fear does not mean
you have no faith. Fear visits everyone.
But make your fear a visitor and not a resident.

MAX LUCADO

God shields us from most of the things we fear,
but when He chooses not to shield us,
He unfailingly allots grace in the measure needed.

ELISABETH ELLIOT

It is good to remind ourselves that
the will of God comes from the heart
of God and that we need not be afraid.

WARREN WIERSBE

A perfect faith would lift us absolutely above fear.

GEORGE MACDONALD

God's power is great enough for our deepest desperation.
You can go on. You can pick up the pieces and start anew.
You can face your fears. You can find peace in the rubble.
There is healing for your soul.

SUZANNE DALE EZELL

The LORD is my light and my salvation—whom should I fear?
The LORD is the stronghold of my life—of whom should I be afraid?

PSALM 27:1 HCSB

BEYOND THE FEAR OF FAILURE

The fear of failure is a powerful motivator, a strong force that can interrupt our plans and derail our dreams. If we're too focused on the uncertainties of the future, we're tempted to "play it safe." Unwilling to move mountains, we fret over molehills. Unwilling to entertain great hopes, we focus on "the unfairness of it all." Unwilling to trust God completely, we take timid half-steps when God intends that we make giant leaps.

Today, ask God for the courage to step beyond the boundaries of your doubts. Ask Him to guide you to a place where you can realize your full potential—a place where you are freed from irrational fears. Ask Him to do His part, and promise Him that you will do your part. Don't ask Him to lead you to a safe place; ask Him to lead you to the right place—and remember: those two places are seldom the same.

MORE THOUGHTS ABOUT THE FEAR OF FAILURE

Risk must be taken because the greatest
hazard in life is to risk nothing.

JOHN MAXWELL

The presence of hope in the invincible
sovereignty of God drives out fear.

JOHN PIPER

Meet your fears with faith.

MAX LUCADO

The Lord Jesus by His Holy Spirit is with me,
and the knowledge of His presence dispels
the darkness and allays any fears.

BILL BRIGHT

There comes a time when we simply have to face the
challenges in our lives and stop backing down.

JOHN ELDREDGE

Finally, all of you be of one mind, having compassion for one another;
love as brothers, be tenderhearted, be courteous.

1 PETER 3:8 NKJV

THE IMPORTANCE OF FELLOWSHIP

God's Word teaches us about the importance of Christian fellowship. The Lord doesn't intend for us to be solitary believers. He wants us to join together as we worship Him and serve His children.

Your association with fellow Christians should be uplifting, encouraging, enlightening, and consistent. In short, fellowship with other believers should be an integral part of your everyday life.

Are you an active member of your own fellowship? Are you a builder of bridges inside the four walls of your church and outside it? Do you contribute to God's glory by contributing your time and your talents to a close-knit band of believers? Hopefully so. The fellowship of believers is intended to be a powerful tool for spreading God's Good News and uplifting His children. And the Lord intends for you to be a fully contributing member of that fellowship. Your intentions should be the same.

SURVIVAL SKILL: FELLOWSHIP

Our love to God is measured by our everyday fellowship
with others and the love it displays.

ANDREW MURRAY

Be united with other Christians. A wall with loose bricks
is not good. The bricks must be cemented together.

CORRIE TEN BOOM

Church-goers are like coals in a fire.
When they cling together, they keep the flame aglow;
when they separate, they die out.

BILLY GRAHAM

The Bible knows nothing of solitary religion.

JOHN WESLEY

Therefore keep in the midst of life.
Do not isolate yourself. Be among men and things,
and among troubles, and difficulties, and obstacles.

HENRY DRUMMOND

37

Let us lay aside every weight and the sin that so easily ensnares us.
Let us run with endurance the race that lies before us,
keeping our eyes on Jesus, the source and perfecter of our faith.

HEBREWS 12:1-2 HCSB

WHAT IS YOUR FOCUS?

What is your focus today? Are you willing to focus your thoughts and energies on God's blessings and upon His plan for your life? Or will you turn your thoughts to other things? Before you answer that question, consider this: The Lord created you in His own image, and He wants you to experience joy and abundance. But He will not force His joy upon you; you must claim it for yourself.

This day—and every day hereafter—is a chance to celebrate the life that God has given you. It is also a chance to give thanks to the One who has offered you more blessings than you can possibly count. So, today, as you seek God's purpose for your life, focus on His love for you. Ask Him for guidance and answer His call. With God as your partner, you'll have every reason to think optimistically about yourself and your world. And you can then share your optimism with others. They'll be better for it, and so will you. But not necessarily in that order.

SURVIVAL SKILL: FOCUS

Let's face it. None of us can do a thousand things
to the glory of God. And, in our own vain attempt to do so,
we stand the risk of forfeiting a precious thing.

BETH MOORE

There is nothing quite as potent as a focused life,
one lived on purpose.

RICK WARREN

Give me a person who says, "This one thing I do,"
and not "These fifty things I dabble in."

D. L. MOODY

Energy and time are limited entities.
Therefore, we need to use them wisely,
focusing on what is truly important.

SARAH YOUNG

It is important to set goals because if you do not have a plan,
a goal, a direction, a purpose, and a focus, you are not
going to accomplish anything for the glory of God.

BILL BRIGHT

38

Then He said to them all, "If anyone desires to come after Me, let him deny himself, and take up his cross daily, and follow Me. For whoever desires to save his life will lose it, but whoever loses his life for My sake will save it."

LUKE 9:23-24 NKJV

FOLLOW HIM

Every day, we're presented with countless opportunities to honor God by following in the footsteps of His Son. But we're sorely tempted to do otherwise. The world is filled to the brim with temptations and distractions that beckon us down a different path.

Elisabeth Elliot had this advice for believers everywhere: "Choose Jesus Christ! Deny yourself, take up the Cross, and follow Him, for the world must be shown. The world must see, in us, a discernible, visible, startling difference."

Today, do your part to take up the cross and follow Him, even if the world encourages you to do otherwise. When you're traveling step-by-step with the Son of God, you're always on the right path.

MORE THOUGHTS ABOUT FOLLOWING CHRIST

A disciple is a follower of Christ. That means you
take on His priorities as your own. His agenda becomes
your agenda. His mission becomes your mission.

CHARLES STANLEY

Christ is not valued at all unless He is valued above all.

ST. AUGUSTINE

Be assured, if you walk with Him and look to Him,
and expect help from Him, He will never fail you.

GEORGE MUELLER

The crucial question for each of us is this:
What do you think of Jesus, and do you yet
have a personal acquaintance with Him?

HANNAH WHITALL SMITH

Of all the things Christ wants for us,
loving Him and focusing our attention on Him
are the most important.

CHARLES STANLEY

39

Blessed are the merciful, because they will be shown mercy.

MATTHEW 5:7 HCSB

BE MERCIFUL

For those who seek to follow in Christ's footsteps, forgiveness isn't optional; it's a commandment. Jesus didn't say, "Forgive when you feel like it," or "Forgive when it's easy." He instructed His followers to forgive quickly, completely, and repeatedly: "Then Peter came to Him and said, 'Lord, how often shall my brother sin against me, and I forgive him? Up to seven times?' Jesus said to him, 'I do not say to you, up to seven times, but up to seventy times seven'" (Matthew 18:21-22 NKJV). Christ's instructions to Peter also apply to each of us. We are commanded—not encouraged, not advised; we are commanded—to forgive and to keep forgiving, even when it's hard.

Bitterness will consume your life if you let it. Hatred will rob you of peace. The search for revenge will leave you frustrated. The only peace that lasts is God's peace, which is only available to those who make the choice to forgive. Sometimes, forgiveness is a hard choice to make, but the rewards are always worth the sacrifice.

MORE THOUGHTS ABOUT FORGIVENESS

Forgiveness does not change the past,
but it does enlarge the future.

DAVID JEREMIAH

Forgiveness is one of the most beautiful words
in the human vocabulary. How much pain could be
avoided if we all learned the meaning of this word!

BILLY GRAHAM

Forgiveness is an act of the will, and the will can function
regardless of the temperature of the heart.

CORRIE TEN BOOM

Forgiveness is God's command.

MARTIN LUTHER

In One bold stroke, forgiveness obliterates the past
and permits us to enter the land of new beginnings.

BILLY GRAHAM

40

But the fruit of the Spirit is love, joy, peace, patience, kindness, goodness, faith, gentleness, self-control. Against such things there is no law.

GALATIANS 5:22-23 HCSB

THE FRUIT OF THE SPIRIT

In the fifth chapter of Galatians, we are also taught that when people live by the Spirit, they will bear "the fruit of the Spirit." But what, exactly, is the fruit of the Spirit? It's a way of behaving, a way of treating other people, a way of showing the world what it means to be a Christian.

Today and every day, will you strive to be patient, joyful, loving, and kind? Will you learn better ways to control negative emotions and impulsive behaviors? And while you're at it, will you be peaceful, gentle, patient, and faithful? If so, you'll show the world what it means to bear the spiritual fruit of our Lord. And you'll demonstrate that your acquaintance with the Master is not a passing fancy; it is, instead, the cornerstone and the touchstone of your life.

MORE THOUGHTS ABOUT
FRUIT OF THE SPIRIT

Though we, as Christians, are like Christ,
having the first fruits of the Spirit, we are unlike Him,
having the remainders of the flesh.

THOMAS WATSON

The Holy Spirit cannot be located as a guest in a house.
He invades everything.

OSWALD CHAMBERS

Some people have received Christ but have
never reached spiritual maturity. We should grow
as Christians every day, and we are not
completely mature until we live in the presence of Christ.

BILLY GRAHAM

The Holy Spirit is like a living and continually flowing
fountain in believers. We have the boundless privilege
of tapping into that fountain every time we pray.

SHIRLEY DOBSON

41

*For I know the thoughts that I think toward you, says the L*ORD*,*
thoughts of peace and not of evil, to give you a future and a hope.
Then you will call upon Me and go and pray to Me, and I will listen to you.

JEREMIAH 29:11-12 NKJV

YOUR VERY BRIGHT FUTURE

If you've entrusted your heart to Christ, your eternal fate is secure and your future is eternally bright. No matter how troublesome your present circumstances may seem, you need not fear because the Lord has promised that you are His now and forever.

Of course, you won't be exempt from the normal challenges of life here on earth. While you're here, you'll probably experience your fair share of disappointments, emergencies, setbacks, and outright failures. But these are only temporary defeats.

Are you willing to place your future in the hands of a loving and all-knowing God? Do you trust in the ultimate goodness of His plan for you? Will you face today's challenges with hope and optimism? You should. After all, God created you for a very important purpose: His purpose. And you still have important work to do: His work. So today, as you live in the present and look to the future, remember that God has a marvelous plan for you. Act—and believe—accordingly.

MORE THOUGHTS ABOUT THE FUTURE

Never be afraid to trust an unknown future to a known God.

CORRIE TEN BOOM

It may be that the day of judgment will
dawn tomorrow; in that case, we shall gladly
stop working for a better future. But not before.

DIETRICH BONHOEFFER

Knowing that your future is absolutely assured
can free you to live abundantly today.

SARAH YOUNG

Our future may look fearfully intimidating,
yet we can look up to the Engineer of the Universe,
confident that nothing escapes His attention
or slips out of the control of those strong hands.

ELISABETH ELLIOT

42

You shall have no other gods before Me.

EXODUS 20:3 NKJV

ALWAYS PUT GOD FIRST

For most of us, these are very busy times. We have obligations at home, at work, at school, or on social media. From the moment we rise until we drift off to sleep at night, we have things to do and people to contact. So how do we find time for God? We must make time for Him, plain and simple. When we put God first, we're blessed. But when we succumb to the pressures and temptations of the world, we inevitably pay a price for our misguided priorities.

In the book of Exodus, God warns that we should put no gods before Him. Yet all too often, we place our Lord in second, third, or fourth place as we focus on other things. When we place our desires for possessions and status above our love for God—or when we yield to the countless distractions that surround us—we forfeit the peace that might otherwise be ours.

In the wilderness, Satan offered Jesus earthly power and unimaginable riches, but Jesus refused. Instead, He chose to worship His heavenly Father. We must do likewise by putting God first and worshiping Him only. God must come first. Always first.

MORE THOUGHTS ABOUT
PUTTING GOD FIRST

The most important thing you must decide
to do every day is put the Lord first.

ELIZABETH GEORGE

Jesus Christ is the first and last, author and finisher,
beginning and end, alpha and omega, and by Him
all other things hold together. He must be first or nothing.
God never comes next!

VANCE HAVNER

Even the most routine part of your day
can be a spiritual act of worship.

SARAH YOUNG

God wants to be in our leisure time as much
as He is in our churches and in our work.

BETH MOORE

Christ is either Lord of all,
or He is not Lord at all.

HUDSON TAYLOR

43

Even when I go through the darkest valley,
I fear no danger, for You are with me.

PSALM 23:4 HCSB

TRUST THE SHEPHERD

In Psalm 23, David teaches us that God is like an attentive shepherd caring for His flock. No wonder these verses have provided hope and comfort for generations of believers.

God watches every step you make and every breath you take, so you need never be afraid. But sometimes, fear has a way of slipping into the minds and hearts of even the most devout Christians—and you are no exception. You know from firsthand experience that life is not always easy. But as a recipient of God's grace, you also know that you are protected by a loving heavenly Father.

On occasion, you will confront circumstances that trouble you to the very core of your soul. When you are afraid, you should trust the Lord. When you are worried, you should turn your concerns over to Him. When you are anxious, you should be still and listen for the quiet assurance of His promises. And then, place your life in His hands. The Lord is your shepherd today and throughout eternity. Trust the Shepherd.

MORE THOUGHTS ABOUT GOD'S COMFORT

The greatest sense of love, which is available
for us at all times, is God's love.

STORMIE OMARTIAN

When God allows extraordinary trials for His people,
He prepares extraordinary comforts for them.

CORRIE TEN BOOM

God is trying to get a message through to you,
and the message is: "Stop depending on inadequate
human resources. Let me handle the matter."

CATHERINE MARSHALL

When I am criticized, injured, or afraid,
there is a Father who is ready to comfort me.

MAX LUCADO

You don't have to be alone in your hurt! Comfort is yours.
Joy is an option. And it's all been made possible by your
Savior. He went without comfort so you might have it.
He postponed joy so you might share in it.
He willingly chose isolation so you might never
be alone in your hurt and sorrow.

JONI EARECKSON TADA

If we say that we have no sin, we deceive ourselves,
and the truth is not in us. If we confess our sins,
He is faithful and just to forgive us our sins
and to cleanse us from all unrighteousness.

1 JOHN 1:8-9 NKJV

GOD'S FORGIVENESS

The Bible promises us that God will forgive our sins if we ask Him. It's our duty to ask; when we've fulfilled that responsibility, He will always fulfill His promise. Yet many of us continue to punish ourselves—with needless guilt and self-loathing—for mistakes that our Creator has long since forgiven and forgotten (Isaiah 43:25).

If you haven't managed to forgive yourself for some past mistake or for a series of poor decisions, it's time to rearrange your thinking. If God has forgiven you, how can you withhold forgiveness from yourself? The answer, of course, is that God's mercy is intended to wash your sins away. That's what the Lord wants, and if you're good enough for Him, you're good enough.

MORE THOUGHTS
ABOUT GOD'S FORGIVENESS

God's mercy is boundless, free, and, through Jesus Christ
our Lord, available to us in our present situation.

A. W. TOZER

God does not wish us to remember
what he is willing to forget.

GEORGE A. BUTTRICK

Forgiveness is an opportunity that God extended
to us on the cross. When we accept His forgiveness
and are willing to forgive ourselves, then we find relief.

BILLY GRAHAM

We cannot out-sin God's ability to forgive us.

BETH MOORE

The most marvelous ingredient in the forgiveness
of God is that he also forgets, the one thing
a human being cannot do. With God,
forgetting is a divine attribute.
God's forgiveness forgets.

OSWALD CHAMBERS

45

*The LORD says, "I will guide you along the best pathway for your life.
I will advise you and watch over you."*

PSALM 32:8 NLT

SEEKING GOD'S GUIDANCE

When we ask for God's guidance, with our hearts and minds open to His direction, He will lead us along a path of His choosing. But for many of us, listening to God is hard. We have so many things we want, and so many needs to pray for, that we spend far more time talking at God than we do listening to Him.

Corrie ten Boom observed, "God's guidance is even more important than common sense. I can declare that the deepest darkness is outshone by the light of Jesus." These words remind us that life is best lived when we seek the Lord's direction early and often.

Our Father has many ways to make Himself known. Our challenge is to make ourselves open to His instruction. So, if you're unsure of your next step, trust God's promises and talk to Him often. When you do, He'll guide your steps today, tomorrow, and forever.

MORE THOUGHTS ABOUT GOD'S GUIDANCE

God never leads us to do anything
that is contrary to the Bible.

BILLY GRAHAM

As you walk through the valley of the unknown,
you will find the footprints of Jesus
both in front of you and beside you.

CHARLES STANLEY

When we are obedient,
God guides our steps and our stops.

CORRIE TEN BOOM

Are you serious about wanting God's guidance
to become a personal reality in your life?
The first step is to tell God that you know you
can't manage your own life; that you need his help.

CATHERINE MARSHALL

The will of God will never take us where
the grace of God cannot sustain us.

BILLY GRAHAM

I know the LORD is always with me.
I will not be shaken, for he is right beside me.

PSALM 16:8 NLT

HE IS HERE

God is everywhere: everywhere you've ever been, everywhere you'll ever be. He is not absent from our world, nor is He absent from your world. God is not "out there"; He is "right here," continuously reshaping His universe, and continuously reshaping the lives of those who dwell in it.

Your Creator is with you always, listening to your thoughts and prayers, watching over your every move. If the demands of everyday life weigh down upon you, you may be tempted to ignore God's presence or—worse yet—to lose faith in His promises. But, when you quiet yourself and acknowledge His presence, God will touch your heart and renew your strength.

Psalm 46:10 remind us to "Be still, and know that I am God." When we do, we can be comforted in the knowledge that God does not love us from a distance. He is not just near. He is here.

MORE THOUGHTS ABOUT GOD'S PRESENCE

God is an infinite circle whose center is everywhere.

St. Augustine

It is God to whom and with whom we travel,
while He is the End of our journey,
He is also at every stopping place.

Elisabeth Elliot

Mark it down. You will never go where God is not.

Max Lucado

Do not limit the limitless God! With Him,
face the future unafraid because you are never alone.

Lettie Cowman

The Lord is the one who travels every mile
of the wilderness way as our leader, cheering us,
supporting and supplying and fortifying us.

Elisabeth Elliot

47

Let us hold fast the confession of our hope without wavering,
for He who promised is faithful.

HEBREWS 10:23 NKJV

HE KEEPS HIS PROMISES

The Bible contains promises upon which you, as a believer, can depend. When the Creator of the universe makes a pledge to you, He will keep it. No exceptions.

You can think of the Bible as a written contract between you and your heavenly Father. When you fulfill your obligations to Him, the Lord will most certainly fulfill His covenant to you.

When we accept Christ into our hearts, God promises us the opportunity to experience contentment, peace, and spiritual abundance. But more importantly, God promises that the priceless gift of eternal life will be ours. These promises should give us comfort. With God on our side, we have absolutely nothing to fear in this world and everything to hope for in the next.

MORE THOUGHTS ABOUT GOD'S PROMISES

Gather the riches of God's promises.
Nobody can take away from you those texts
from the Bible which you have learned by heart.

CORRIE TEN BOOM

The Bible is God's book of promises, and unlike
the books of man, it does not change or go out of date.

BILLY GRAHAM

Beloved, God's promises can never fail to be accomplished,
and those who patiently wait can never be disappointed,
for a believing faith leads to realization.

LETTIE COWMAN

Don't let obstacles along the road to eternity
shake your confidence in God's promises.

DAVID JEREMIAH

Let God's promises shine on your problems.

CORRIE TEN BOOM

48

*The Lord is my shepherd; I shall not want. He makes me to lie down
in green pastures; He leads me beside the still waters. He restores my soul.*

PSALM 23:1-3 NKJV

GOD IS YOUR ULTIMATE PROTECTION

In a world filled with dangers and temptations, God is the ultimate armor. In a world filled with misleading messages, God's Word is the ultimate truth. In a world filled with more frustrations than we can count, God's Son offers the ultimate peace.

The Lord is our greatest refuge. When every earthly support system fails, He remains steadfast, and His love remains unchanged. When we encounter life's inevitable disappointments and setbacks, the Father remains faithful. When we suffer, He is always with us, always ready to respond to our prayers, always working in us and through us to turn tragedy into triumph.

Thankfully, even when there's nowhere else to turn, You can turn your thoughts and prayers to the Lord, and He will respond. In every emergency, God will stand by you. Your job, of course, is to return the favor and stand by Him today, tomorrow, and every day of your life.

SURVIVAL SKILL: GOD'S PROTECTION

A mighty fortress is our God, a bulwark never failing,
our helper he amid the flood of mortal ills prevailing.

MARTIN LUTHER

Measure the size of the obstacles against the size of God.

BETH MOORE

Only believe, don't fear. Our Master, Jesus,
always watches over us, and no matter what
the persecution, Jesus will surely overcome it.

LOTTIE MOON

The safest place in all the world
is in the will of God, and the safest protection
in all the world is the name of God.

WARREN WIERSBE

As you walk through the valley of the unknown,
you will find the footprints of Jesus
both in front of you and beside you.

CHARLES STANLEY

49

God is our refuge and strength, a very present help in trouble.

PSALM 46:1 NKJV

HE WILL STRENGTHEN YOU

If you're enduring tough times, or if you're reeling from an unexpected setback, you may be feeling emotionally drained or physically exhausted. If so, there's a place you can turn for strength; you can turn your thoughts—and lift your prayers—to God. When you do, you can be sure that the loving heart of God is sufficient to meet any challenge, including yours.

God loves you. In times of trouble, He will comfort you; in times of sorrow, He will dry your tears. When you are lonely or discouraged, the Lord is as near as your next breath. He stands at the door of your heart and waits. Welcome Him in and allow Him to rule. And then, accept the strength, the protection, the peace, and the abundance that only He can give.

SURVIVAL SKILL: GOD'S STRENGTH

God will give us the strength and resources we need to live
through any situation in life that He ordains.

BILLY GRAHAM

Our Lord never drew power from Himself;
He drew it always from His Father.

OSWALD CHAMBERS

God is sufficient for all our needs,
for every problem, for every difficulty,
for every broken heart, for every human sorrow.

PETER MARSHALL

God's all-sufficiency is a major.
Your inability is a minor.
Major in majors, not in minors.

CORRIE TEN BOOM

We shouldn't think about ourselves and how weak we are.
We should think about God and how strong He is.

BILLY GRAHAM

50

Humble yourselves, therefore, under the mighty hand of God,
so that He may exalt you at the proper time,
casting all your care upon Him, because He cares about you.

1 PETER 5:6-7 HCSB

HE CARES

God's Word promises that He will support you in good times and comfort you in hard times. The Creator of the universe stands ready to give you the strength to meet any challenge and the courage to face any adversity. When you ask for God's help, He responds in His own way and at His own appointed hour. But make no mistake: He always responds.

In a world brimming with dangers and temptations, God is the ultimate armor. In a world saturated with misleading messages, God's Word is the ultimate truth. In a world filled with frustrations and distractions, God's Son offers the ultimate peace.

Today, as you encounter the inevitable challenges of everyday life, remember that your heavenly Father never leaves you, not even for a moment. He's always available, always ready to listen, always ready to lead. When you make a habit of talking to Him early and often, He'll guide you and comfort you every day of your life.

MORE THOUGHTS ABOUT GOD'S SUPPORT

Put your hand into the hand of God.
He gives the calmness and serenity of heart and soul.

LETTIE COWMAN

Measure the size of the obstacles
against the size of God.

BETH MOORE

The knowledge that we are never alone
calms the troubled sea of our lives
and speaks peace to our souls.

A. W. TOZER

The will of God is either a burden
we carry or a power which carries us.

CORRIE TEN BOOM

When once we are assured that God is good,
then there can be nothing left to fear.

HANNAH WHITALL SMITH

To everything there is a season, a time for every purpose under heaven.

ECCLESIASTES 3:1 NKJV

TRUST GOD'S TIMING

If you're like most people, you're in a hurry. You know precisely what you want, and you know precisely when you want it: as soon as possible. Because your time on earth is limited, you may feel a sense of urgency. God does not. There is no panic in heaven.

Our heavenly Father, in His infinite wisdom, operates according to His own timetable, not ours. He has plans that we cannot see and purposes that we cannot know. He has created a world that unfolds according to His own schedule. Thank goodness! After all, He is omniscient; He is trustworthy; and He knows what's best for us.

If you've been waiting impatiently for the Lord to answer your prayers, it's time to put a stop to all that needless worry. You can be sure that God will answer your prayers when the time is right. You job is to keep praying—and working—until He does.

MORE THOUGHTS ABOUT GOD'S TIMING

We must learn to move according to the timetable
of the Timeless One, and to be at peace.

ELISABETH ELLIOT

Waiting on God brings us to
the journey's end quicker than our feet.

LETTIE COWMAN

The Christian's journey through life
isn't a sprint but a marathon.

BILLY GRAHAM

Teach us, O Lord, the disciplines of patience,
for to wait is often harder than to work.

PETER MARSHALL

We often hear about waiting on God,
which actually means that He is waiting until
we are ready. There is another side, however.
When we wait for God, we are waiting until He is ready.

LETTIE COWMAN

52

For you are saved by grace through faith, and this is not from yourselves;
it is God's gift—not from works, so that no one can boast.

EPHESIANS 2:8-9 HCSB

THE GIFT OF GRACE

God's grace is sufficient to meet every our every need. No matter our circumstances, no matter our personal histories, the Lord's precious gifts are always available. All we need do is to form a personal, life-altering relationship with His only begotten Son, and we're secure, now and forever.

Grace is unearned, undeserved favor from God. His grace is available to each of us. No sin is too terrible, no behavior too outrageous, to separate us from God's love. We are saved by grace through faith. Jesus paid for our sins on the cross, and when we trust Him completely, God pronounces us "not guilty" of our transgressions.

Have you accepted Christ as your king, your shepherd, and your savior? If so, you are protected now and forever. If not, this moment is the appropriate time to trust God's Son and accept God's grace. It's never too soon, or too late, to welcome Jesus into your heart.

MORE THOUGHTS ABOUT GRACE

Grace is the free, undeserved goodness
and favor of God to mankind.

MATTHEW HENRY

The will of God will never take us where
the grace of God cannot sustain us.

BILLY GRAHAM

Immerse yourself in the curriculum of grace.

MAX LUCADO

God's grace is His unmerited favor toward
the unworthy, by which He delivers them
from condemnation and death.

JOHN MACARTHUR

God's grace is just the right amount of just
the right quality arriving as if from
nowhere at just the right time.

BILL BRIGHT

53

In everything give thanks; for this is the will of God in Christ Jesus for you.

1 Thessalonians 5:18 NKJV

BE THANKFUL

When we consider God's blessings and the sacrifices of His Son, just how thankful should we be? Should we praise our Creator once a day? Are two prayers enough? Is it sufficient that we thank our heavenly Father at mealtimes and bedtimes? The answer, of course, is no. When we consider how richly we have been blessed, now and forever—and when we consider the price Christ paid on the cross—it becomes clear that we should offer many prayers of thanks throughout the day. But all too often, amid the hustle of daily life, we forget to pause and praise the Giver of all good gifts.

Our lives expand or contract in proportion to our gratitude. When we are appropriately grateful for God's countless blessings, we experience His peace. But if we ignore His gifts, we invite stress, anxiety, and sadness into our lives.

Throughout this day, pause and say silent prayers of thanks. When you do, you'll discover that a grateful heart reaps countless blessings that a hardened heart will never know.

SURVIVAL SKILL: GRATITUDE

How ridiculous to grasp for future gifts when today's
is set before you. Receive today's gift gratefully,
unwrapping it tenderly and delving into its depths.

SARAH YOUNG

Thanksgiving or complaining—these words express two
contrasting attitudes of the souls of God's children.
The soul that gives thanks can find comfort in everything;
the soul that complains can find comfort in nothing.

HANNAH WHITALL SMITH

God is in control, and therefore in everything
I can give thanks—not because of the situation
but because of the One who directs and rules over it.

KAY ARTHUR

It is always possible to be thankful for what is given
rather than to complain about what is not given.
One or the other becomes a habit of life.

ELISABETH ELLIOT

Fill up the spare moments of your life
with praise and thanksgiving.

SARAH YOUNG

54

Weeping may endure for a night, but joy comes in the morning.

PSALM 30:5 NKJV

BEYOND GRIEF

If you're experiencing the pains of a significant loss, God's promises offer comfort. And if you'd like to experience God's peace, Bible study can help provide it.

Warren Wiersbe observed, "When the child of God looks into the Word of God, he sees the Son of God. And, he is transformed by the Spirit of God to share in the glory of God." God's Holy Word is, indeed, a life-changing, spirit-lifting, one-of-a-kind treasure. And it's up to you—and only you—to use it that way.

Jonathan Edwards advised, "Be assiduous in reading the Holy Scriptures. This is the fountain whence all knowledge in divinity must be derived. Therefore let not this treasure lie by you neglected." God's Holy Word is, indeed, a priceless, one-of-a-kind treasure. Handle it with care, but more importantly, handle it every day, especially when you're recovering from a painful loss.

MORE THOUGHTS ABOUT GRIEF

If there is something we need more than anything
else during grief, it is a friend who stands with us,
who doesn't leave us. Jesus is that friend.

BILLY GRAHAM

God is sufficient for all our needs,
for every problem, for every difficulty,
for every broken heart, for every human sorrow.

PETER MARSHALL

Despair is always the gateway of faith.

OSWALD CHAMBERS

God has enough grace to solve
every dilemma you face,
wipe every tear you cry,
and answer every question you ask.

MAX LUCADO

Your greatest ministry will most likely
come out of your greatest hurt.

RICK WARREN

Guard your heart above all else, for it is the source of life.

PROVERBS 4:23 HCSB

GUARD YOUR HEART

God loves you; He cares for you; and He wants the very best for you. The Lord knows that your adversary is near, and He wants you to guard against temptations that can do you harm. So God wants you to guard your heart.

Every day, you're faced with an array of choices—more choices than you can count. You can do the right thing, or not. You can be prudent, or not. You can be humble, kind, and obedient. Or not.

Today, the world will offer you countless opportunities to let down your guard and, by doing so, make needless mistakes that may injure you and your loved ones. So be watchful. Guard your heart by giving it to your heavenly Father; it is safe with Him.

MORE THOUGHTS ABOUT
GUARDING YOUR HEART

Our fight is not against any physical enemy; it is against
organizations and powers that are spiritual. We must struggle
against sin all our lives, but we are assured we will win.

CORRIE TEN BOOM

The insight that relates to God comes from purity of heart,
not from clearness of intellect.

OSWALD CHAMBERS

There is no neutral ground in the universe:
every square inch, every split second, is claimed by God
and counterclaimed by Satan.

C. S. LEWIS

No matter how many pleasures Satan offers you,
his ultimate intention is to ruin you.
Your destruction is his highest priority.

ERWIN LUTZER

Our battles are first won or lost in the secret places of our
will in God's presence, never in full view of the world.

OSWALD CHAMBERS

Let not your heart be troubled: ye believe in God, believe also in me.
In my Father's house are many mansions: if it were not so,
I would have told you. I go to prepare a place for you.
And if I go and prepare a place for you, I will come again,
and receive you unto myself; that where I am, there ye may be also.

JOHN 14:1-3 KJV

HEAVEN IS YOUR REAL HOME

Sometimes life's unexpected emergencies are easier to tolerate when we remind ourselves that this earth is not our home. For believers, death is not an ending; it is a beginning. And the grave is not a final resting place; it is a place of transition.

If you've committed your life to Christ, your time here on earth is merely a preparation for a far better life to come: your eternal life in heaven. So, while this world can be a place of hardship and suffering, you can be comforted in the knowledge that the Lord offers you a permanent home that is free from sorrow and pain. Please take God at His word. When you do, you can withstand any problem, knowing that your troubles are temporary, but that heaven is not.

MORE THOUGHTS ABOUT HEAVEN

This world is not our home;
our citizenship is in heaven.

BILLY GRAHAM

The end will be glorious beyond our wildest dreams—
for those who put their trust in Him.

ELISABETH ELLIOT

Earth's best is only a dim reflection
and a preliminary rendering of the glory
that will one day be revealed.

JONI EARECKSON TADA

If you are a Christian, you are not a citizen
of this world trying to get to heaven;
you are a citizen of heaven making
your way through this world.

VANCE HAVNER

When you speak of heaven, let your face light up.

C. H. SPURGEON

*We have this hope as an anchor for our lives, safe and secure.
It enters the inner sanctuary behind the curtain.*

HEBREWS 6:19 HCSB

NEVER LOSE HOPE

Despite God's love, and despite His countless blessings, we frail human beings can still lose hope from time to time. When we do, we need the support of Christian friends, the life-changing power of prayer, and the healing truth of God's Holy Word.

This world can be a place of pain and heartache, but as a believer, you are protected. God has made many promises to you, and He intends to keep every single one of them. Since the Father always God keeps His promises, you are safe, now and forever. Your security is assured through His faithfulness.

SURVIVAL SKILL: HOPE

The presence of hope in the invincible
sovereignty of God drives out fear.

JOHN PIPER

Of course you will encounter trouble.
But behold a God of power who can
take any evil and turn it into a door of hope.

CATHERINE MARSHALL

Jesus gives us hope because He keeps us company,
has a vision and knows the way we should go.

MAX LUCADO

The earth's troubles fade in the light of heaven's hope.

BILLY GRAHAM

If your hopes are being disappointed just now,
it means that they are being purified.

OSWALD CHAMBERS

58

The greatest among you will be your servant. For those who exalt themselves will be humbled, and those who humble themselves will be exalted.

MATTHEW 23:11-12 NIV

BE HUMBLE

We humans are often tempted by a dangerous, debilitating sin: pride. Even though God's Word clearly warns us that pride is hazardous to our spiritual health, we're still tempted to brag about our accomplishments and overstate them. We're tempted to puff ourselves up by embellishing our victories and concealing our defeats. But in truth, all of us are mere mortals who have many more reasons to be humble than prideful.

As Christians who have been saved, not by our own good works but by God's grace, how can we be prideful? The answer, of course, is that if we are honest with ourselves and with our God we simply can't be boastful. We must, instead, be filled with humble appreciation for the things God has done. Our good works are miniscule compared to His. Whatever happens, the Lord deserves the credit, not us. And, if we're wise, we'll give Him all the credit He deserves.

SURVIVAL SKILL: HUMILITY

Pride builds walls between people,
humility builds bridges.

RICK WARREN

Faith itself cannot be strong where humility is weak.

C. H. SPURGEON

God measures people by the small dimensions
of humility and not by the bigness of their achievements
or the size of their capabilities.

BILLY GRAHAM

The holy man is the most humble man you can meet.

OSWALD CHAMBERS

Humility is not thinking less of yourself,
it's thinking of yourself less.

RICK WARREN

59

Enthusiasm without knowledge is not good.
If you act too quickly, you might make a mistake.

PROVERBS 19:2 NCV

SLOW DOWN

The Bible teaches us to be cautious, to be careful, and to be prudent. But the world often tempts us to be imprudent and impetuous. The world is brimming with temptations that encourage us to behave recklessly, without preparation or forethought. These are temptations that we must resist.

So the next time you're tempted to make an impulsive decision, slow down, think things over, and contemplate the consequences of your behavior before you act, rather than after. When you make a habit of thinking first and acting second, you'll be comforted in the knowledge that you're incorporating God's wisdom into the fabric of your life. And you'll earn the rewards that the Creator inevitably bestows upon those who take the time to look—and to think—before they leap.

MORE THOUGHTS ABOUT IMPULSIVITY

We must learn to wait. There is grace supplied
to the one who waits.

LETTIE COWMAN

Patience is the companion of wisdom.

ST. AUGUSTINE

Zeal without knowledge is fire without light.

THOMAS FULLER

Nothing is more terrible than activity without insight.

THOMAS CARLYLE

In times of uncertainty, wait. Always,
if you have any doubt, wait. Do not force yourself
to any action. If you have a restraint in your spirit,
wait until all is clear, and do not go against it.

LETTIE COWMAN

*These things I have spoken to you, that My joy may remain in you,
and that your joy may be full.*

JOHN 15:11 NKJV

BE JOYFUL

The joy that the world offers is fleeting and incomplete: here today, gone tomorrow, not coming back anytime soon. But God's joy is different. His joy has staying power. In fact, it's a gift that never stops giving to those who welcome His Son into their hearts.

Psalm 100 reminds us to celebrate the lives that God has given us: "Shout for joy to the LORD, all the earth. Worship the LORD with gladness; come before Him with joyful songs." (vv. 1-2 NIV). Yet sometimes, amid the inevitable complications and predicaments that are woven into the fabric of everyday life, we forget to rejoice. Instead of celebrating life, we complain about it. This is an understandable mistake, but a mistake nonetheless. As Christians, we are called by our Creator to live joyfully and abundantly. To do otherwise is to squander His spiritual gifts.

This day and every day, Christ offers you His peace and His joy. Accept it and share it with others, just as He has shared His joy with you.

MORE THOUGHTS ABOUT JOY

Joy is the great note all throughout the Bible.

OSWALD CHAMBERS

Joy is the direct result of having
God's perspective on our daily lives
and the effect of loving our Lord
enough to obey His commands
and trust His promises.

BILL BRIGHT

Joy comes not from what
we have but what we are.

C. H. SPURGEON

Joy is the settled assurance that God
is in control of all the details of my life,
the quiet confidence that ultimately
everything is going to be all right,
and the determined choice
to praise God in all things.

KAY WARREN

Joy is the serious business of heaven.

C. S. LEWIS

61

Speak, LORD. I am your servant and I am listening.

1 SAMUEL 3:10 NCV

LISTENING TO GOD

God speaks to us in different ways at different times. Sometimes He speaks loudly and clearly. But more often, He speaks in a quiet voice—and if you are wise, you will be listening carefully when He does. To do so, you must carve out quiet moments each day to study His Word and to sense His direction.

Are you willing to pray sincerely and then to wait quietly for God's response? Can you quiet yourself long enough to listen to your conscience? Are you attuned to the subtle guidance of your intuition? Hopefully so. Usually God refrains from sending His messages on stone tablets or city billboards. More often, He communicates in subtler ways. If you sincerely desire to hear His voice, you must listen carefully, and you must do so in the silent corners of your quiet, willing heart.

MORE THOUGHTS ABOUT
LISTENING TO GOD

When God speaks to us, He should have our full attention.

BILLY GRAHAM

If you, too, will learn to wait upon God,
to get alone with Him, and remain silent so that you can
hear His voice when He is ready to speak to you,
what a difference it will make in you life!

KAY ARTHUR

Deep within the center of the soul is a chamber of peace
where God lives and where, if we will enter it and quiet all
the other sounds, we can hear His gentle whisper.

LETTIE COWMAN

Prayer begins by talking to God, but it ends
in listening to him. In the face of Absolute Truth,
silence is the soul's language.

FULTON J. SHEEN

God's voice is still and quiet and easily buried
under an avalanche of clamor.

CHARLES STANLEY

62

*Jesus said to him, "'You shall love the LORD your God
with all your heart, with all your soul, and with all your mind.'
This is the first and great commandment."*

MATTHEW 22:37-38 NKJV

LOVING GOD

The Bible teaches us to love God with all our hearts. But sometimes, we fall short of the mark. Sometimes, despite our best intentions, we become embittered with ourselves, with our neighbors, or with our Creator.

If we are to please God, we must cleanse ourselves of the negative feelings that separate us from others and from Him. So today and every day, fill your heart with love. Don't yield to bitterness. And praise the Son of God who, in His infinite wisdom, made love His greatest commandment. Put God first in your life and in your heart. He deserves your adoration, and you deserve the experience of giving it to Him.

MORE THOUGHTS ABOUT LOVING GOD

I love Him because He first loved me, and He still does
love me, and He will love me forever and ever.

BILL BRIGHT

Loving Him means the thankful acceptance
of all things that His love has appointed.

ELISABETH ELLIOT

When an honest soul can get still before the living Christ,
we can still hear Him say simply and clearly, "Love the Lord
your God with all your heart and with all your soul and with
all your mind...and love one another as I have loved you."

GLORIA GAITHER

Joy is a by-product not of happy circumstances,
education or talent, but of a healthy relationship with God
and a determination to love Him no matter what.

BARBARA JOHNSON

God is so inconceivably good.
He's not looking for perfection.
He already saw it in Christ.
He's looking for affection.

BETH MOORE

63

But Jesus looked at them and said, "With men this is impossible, but with God all things are possible."

MATTHEW 19:26 HCSB

ALL THINGS ARE POSSIBLE

God's power has no limitations. He is not restrained by the laws of nature because He created those laws. At any time, at any place, under any set of circumstances, He can accomplish anything He chooses. The things that seem miraculous to us are, to Him, expressions of His power and His love.

Do you expect God to work miracles in your own life? You should. From the moment He created our universe out of nothingness, the Lord has made a habit of doing miraculous things. And He's still working miracles today.

With God nothing is impossible. His wondrous works come in all shapes and sizes, so keep your eyes and your heart open. Somewhere, a miracle is about to happen, and it might just happen to you.

MORE THOUGHTS ABOUT MIRACLES

Consider Jesus. Know Jesus. Learn what kind of Person
it is you say you trust and love and worship. Soak in the
shadow of Jesus. Saturate your soul with the ways of Jesus.
Watch Him. Listen to Him. Stand in awe of Him.

JOHN PIPER

Miracles are not contrary to nature,
but only contrary to what we know about nature.

ST. AUGUSTINE

God is able to do what we can't do.

BILLY GRAHAM

Are you looking for a miracle?
If you keep your eyes
wide open and trust in God,
you won't have to look very far.

MARIE T. FREEMAN

God's specialty is raising dead things to life
and making impossible things possible.
You don't have the need that exceeds His power.

BETH MOORE

64

The one who conceals his sins will not prosper,
but whoever confesses and renounces them will find mercy.

PROVERBS 28:13 HCSB

WHEN YOU MAKE A MISTAKE

No one—none—is perfect; we all make mistakes. The question, then, is not whether we'll make mistakes, but what we'll do about them. If we focus on covering up instead of fixing, we invite even more troubles. But if we learn from our mistakes and make amends whenever possible, God will help us make use of our setbacks.

Have you recently made a mistake that caused trouble, disappointment, or heartbreak? If so, look for the lesson that the Lord is trying to teach you. Instead of grumbling about life's sad state of affairs, learn what needs to be learned, change what needs to be changed, and move on. View every major setback as an opportunity to reassess God's will for your life. And while you're at it, consider your mistakes to be powerful opportunities to learn more about yourself, your circumstances, and your world.

Everybody (including you) makes mistakes. Your job is to make them only once. And with God's help, you can do it.

MORE THOUGHTS ABOUT MISTAKES

God is able to take mistakes, when they are
committed to Him, and make of them something
for our good and for His glory.

RUTH BELL GRAHAM

By the mercy of God, we may repent a wrong choice
and alter the consequences by making a right choice.

A. W. TOZER

Mistakes offer the possibility for redemption
and a new start in God's kingdom. No matter what
you're guilty of, God can restore your innocence.

BARBARA JOHNSON

Every misfortune, every failure,
every loss may be transformed. God has the power
to transform all misfortunes into "God-sends."

LETTIE COWMAN

It is human to err, but it is devilish
to remain willfully in error.

ST. AUGUSTINE

65

Therefore if anyone is in Christ, he is a new creature;
the old things passed away; behold, new things have come.

2 Corinthians 5:17 NASB

A FRESH START

Our heavenly Father has the power to make all things new. When we go to Him with sincere hearts and willing hands, He renews our spirits and redirects our steps.

Are you searching for a new path? If so, the Lord is waiting patiently to give you a fresh start. He's prepared to help you change your thoughts, rearrange your priorities and transform your life. But it doesn't stop there. He's also made a standing offer to forgive your sins, to forget your failings, and to protect you throughout all eternity. All you must do is ask.

Are you ready for a new beginning? If so, today is the perfect day to claim it by making God your partner in every endeavor. He can make all things new, including you.

MORE THOUGHTS ABOUT NEW BEGINNINGS

God specializes in giving people a fresh start.

RICK WARREN

What saves a man is to take a step.
Then another step.

C. S. LEWIS

Each day you must say to yourself,
"Today I am going to begin."

JEAN PIERRE DE CAUSSADE

The best preparation for the future
is the present well seen to, and the last duty done.

GEORGE MACDONALD

Are you in earnest? Seize this very minute.
What you can do, or dream you can, begin it.
Boldness has genius, power, and magic in it.

GOETHE

66

This is how we are sure that we have come to know Him:
by keeping His commands.

1 JOHN 2:3 HCSB

OBEY HIM

God's instructions to mankind are contained in a book like no other: the Holy Bible. When we obey God's commandments and listen carefully to the conscience He has placed in our hearts, we are secure. But if we disobey our Creator, if we choose to ignore the teachings and the warnings of His Word, we do so at great peril.

Susanna Wesley said, "There are two things to do about the Gospel: believe it and behave it." Her words serve as a powerful reminder that, as Christians, we are called to take God's promises seriously and to live in accordance with His teachings.

God gave us His commandments for a reason: so that we might obey them and be blessed. Yet we live in a world that presents us with countless temptations to stray far from His path. It is our responsibility to resist those temptations with vigor. Obedience isn't just the best way to experience the full measure of God's blessings; it's the only way.

SURVIVAL SKILL: OBEDIENCE

The golden rule for understanding
in spiritual matters is not intellect, but obedience.

OSWALD CHAMBERS

Obedience is a foundational stepping-stone
on the path of God's will.

ELIZABETH GEORGE

Obedience is the key to every door.

GEORGE MACDONALD

Faith and obedience are bound up
in the same bundle. He that obeys God,
trusts God; and he that trusts God, obeys God.

C. H. SPURGEON

God has laid down spiritual laws which,
if obeyed, bring harmony and fulfillment,
but, if disobeyed, bring discord and disorder.

BILLY GRAHAM

67

My cup runs over. Surely goodness and mercy shall follow me
all the days of my life; and I will dwell in the house of the LORD forever.

PSALM 23:5-6 NKJV

OPTIMISTIC CHRISTIANITY

Are you a passionate Christian who expects God to do big things in your life and in the lives of those around you? If you're a thinking Christian, you have every reason to be confident about your future here on earth and your eternal future in heaven. As English clergyman William Ralph Inge observed, "No Christian should be a pessimist, for Christianity is a system of radical optimism." Inge's observation is true, of course, but sometimes, you may find yourself caught up in the inevitable complications of everyday living. When you find yourself fretting about the inevitable ups and downs of life here on earth, it's time to slow down, collect yourself, refocus your thoughts, and count your blessings.

God has made promises to you, and He will most certainly keep every one of them. So you have every reason to be an optimist and no legitimate reason to ever abandon hope.

Today, trust your hopes, not your fears. And while you're at it, take time to celebrate God's blessings. His gifts are too numerous to calculate and too glorious to imagine. But it never hurts to try.

SURVIVAL SKILL: OPTIMISM

Positive thinking will let you do everything
better than negative thinking will.

ZIG ZIGLAR

When you have vision it affects your attitude.
Your attitude is optimistic rather than pessimistic.

CHARLES SWINDOLL

Two types of voices command your attention today.
Negative ones fill your mind with doubt, bitterness,
and fear. Positive ones purvey hope and strength.
Which one will you choose to heed?

MAX LUCADO

No more imperfect thoughts. No more sad memories.
No more ignorance. My redeemed body will have
a redeemed mind. Grant me a foretaste of that
perfect mind as you mirror your thoughts in me today.

JONI EARECKSON TADA

68

*Patient endurance is what you need now, so that you will continue
to do God's will. Then you will receive all that he has promised.*

HEBREWS 10:36 NLT

THE POWER OF PATIENCE

Time and again, the Bible promises us that patience is its
own reward, but not its only reward. Yet we human beings are,
by nature, an impatient lot. We know what we want and we
know when we want it: right now!

We live in an imperfect world inhabited by imperfect
family members, imperfect friends, imperfect acquaintances,
and imperfect strangers. Sometimes we inherit troubles from
these imperfect people, and sometimes we create troubles for
ourselves. In either case, what's required is patience—patience
for other people's shortcomings as well as our own.

Proverbs 16:32 teaches, "Better to be patient than powerful;
better to have self-control than to conquer a city" (NLT). But,
for most of us, waiting patiently is hard. We are fallible beings
who want things today, not tomorrow. Still, God instructs us
to be patient, and that's what we must do. It's the peaceful way
to live.

SURVIVAL SKILL: PATIENCE

Patience is the companion of wisdom.

St. Augustine

Bear with the faults of others as you
would have them bear with yours.

Phillips Brooks

Patience graciously, compassionately,
and with understanding, judges the faults
of others without unjust criticism.

Billy Graham

Today, take a complicated situation and with time,
patience, and a smile, turn it into something positive—
for you and for others.

Joni Eareckson Tada

Frustration is not the will of God. There is time
to do anything and everything that God wants us to do.

Elisabeth Elliot

*And the peace of God, which surpasses every thought, will guard your hearts
and your minds in Christ Jesus. Finally brothers, whatever is true,
whatever is honorable, whatever is just, whatever is pure,
whatever is lovely, whatever is commendable—if there is any
moral excellence and if there is any praise—dwell on these things.*

PHILIPPIANS 4:7-8 HCSB

FINDING GENUINE PEACE

Peace. It's such a beautiful word. It conveys images of serenity, contentment, and freedom from the trials and tribulations of everyday existence. Peace means freedom from conflict, freedom from inner turmoil, and freedom from worry. Peace is such a beautiful concept that advertisers and marketers attempt to sell it with images of relaxed vacationers lounging on the beach or happy senior citizens celebrating on the golf course. But contrary to the implied claims of modern media, real peace, genuine peace, isn't for sale. At any price.

Have you discovered the genuine peace that can be yours through Christ? Or are you still scurrying after the illusion of peace that the world promises but cannot deliver? If you've turned things over to Jesus, you'll be blessed now and forever. So what are you waiting for? Let Him rule your heart and your

thoughts, beginning now. When you do, you'll experience the
peace that only He can give.

MORE THOUGHTS ABOUT PEACE

Deep within the center of the soul is a chamber of peace
where God lives and where, if we will enter it and quiet
all the other sounds, we can hear His gentle whisper.

LETTIE COWMAN

Peace does not mean to be in a place where there is no noise,
trouble, or hard work. Peace means to be in the midst
of all those things and still be calm in your heart.

CATHERINE MARSHALL

In the center of a hurricane there is absolute
quiet and peace. There is no safer place
than in the center of the will of God.

CORRIE TEN BOOM

God's power is great enough for our deepest desperation.
You can go on. You can pick up the pieces and start anew.
You can face your fears. You can find peace in the rubble.
There is healing for your soul.

SUZANNE DALE EZELL

For am I now trying to win the favor of people, or God?
Or am I striving to please people? If I were still trying
to please people, I would not be a slave of Christ.

GALATIANS 1:10 HCSB

PLEASE HIM

Sometimes, because you're an imperfect human being, you may become so wrapped up in meeting society's expectations that you fail to focus on God's expectations. To do so is a mistake of major proportions; don't make it. Instead, seek God's guidance in every aspect of your life. And when it comes to matters of conscience, seek approval not from your peers, but from your Creator.

Whom will you try to please today: God or man? Your primary obligation is not to please imperfect friends or casual acquaintances. Your obligation is to meet the Lord's expectations. So turn your concerns over to Him—prayerfully, earnestly, and often. Then listen for His answers, and trust the answers He gives.

MORE THOUGHTS ABOUT PLEASING GOD

An ongoing relationship with God through His Word is
essential to the Christian's consistent victory.

BETH MOORE

To yield to God means to belong to God,
and to belong to God means to have all His infinite power.
To belong to God means to have all.

HANNAH WHITALL SMITH

Loving God—really loving Him—means living out
His commands no matter what the cost.

CHARLES COLSON

Give me grace ever to desire and to will what is most
acceptable to thee and most pleasing in thy sight.

THOMAS À KEMPIS

We may blunder on for years thinking we know
a great deal about Him, and then, perhaps suddenly,
we catch a sight of Him as He is revealed in the face
of Jesus Christ, and we discover the real God.

HANNAH WHITALL SMITH

71

*Praise the LORD! Oh, give thanks to the LORD,
for He is good! For His mercy endures forever.*

PSALM 106:1 NKJV

PRAISE HIM

The Bible teaches us to praise God, but sometimes we become so preoccupied with the emergencies and demands of everyday life that we forget to say "Thank You" to the Giver of all good gifts.

Praise and worship should never be relegated to Sunday mornings; instead, we should weave prayer and thanksgiving into every aspect of everyday life.

Theologian Wayne Oates once admitted, "Many of my prayers are made with my eyes open. You see, it seems I'm always praying about something, and it's not always convenient—or safe—to close my eyes." Dr. Oates understood that God always hears our prayers and that the relative position of our eyelids is of no concern to Him.

If you sincerely desire to be a worthy servant of the One who has given you eternal love and eternal life, praise Him for who He is and for what He has done for you. Don't just praise

Him on Sunday. Praise Him throughout the day, every day, for as long as you live…And then for all eternity.

SURVIVAL SKILL: PRAISE

Two wings are necessary to lift our souls toward God: prayer and praise. Prayer asks. Praise accepts the answer.

LETTIE COWMAN

This is my story, this is my song,
praising my Savior, all the day long.

FANNY CROSBY

Preoccupy my thoughts with
your praise beginning today.

JONI EARECKSON TADA

The time for universal praise is sure to come some day.
Let us begin to do our part now.

HANNAH WHITALL SMITH

The best moment to praise God
is always the present one.

MARIE T. FREEMAN

72

Rejoice always, pray without ceasing, in everything give thanks;
for this is the will of God in Christ Jesus for you.

1 THESSALONIANS 5:16-18 NKJV

THE POWER OF PRAYER

Prayer is a powerful tool that you can use to change your world and change yourself. God hears every prayer and responds in His own way and according to His own timetable. When you make a habit of consulting Him about everything, He'll guide you along a path of His choosing, which, by the way, is the path you should take. And when you petition Him for strength, He'll give you the courage to face any problem and the power to meet any challenge. So today, instead of turning things over in your mind, turn them over to God in prayer. Take your concerns to the Lord and leave them there. Your heavenly Father is listening, and He wants to hear from you. Now.

SURVIVAL SKILL: PRAYER

Prayer is our lifeline to God.

BILLY GRAHAM

Any concern that is too small to be turned into a prayer
is too small to be made into a burden.

CORRIE TEN BOOM

Two wings are necessary to lift our souls toward God:
prayer and praise. Prayer asks. Praise accepts the answer.

LETTIE COWMAN

Don't pray when you feel like it.
Have an appointment with the Lord and keep it.

CORRIE TEN BOOM

It is impossible to overstate the need for prayer
in the fabric of family life.

JAMES DOBSON

73

People who do what is right may have many problems,
but the LORD will solve them all.

PSALM 34:19 NCV

SOLVING PROBLEMS

So here's a riddle: What is it that is too unimportant to pray about yet too big for God to handle? The answer, of course, is: nothing. Yet sometimes, when the demands of everyday life seem overwhelming, we may spend more time worrying about our troubles than praying about them. And we may spend more time fretting about our problems than solving them. A far better strategy is to pray as if everything depended entirely upon God and to work as if everything depended entirely upon us.

What we see as problems God sees as opportunities. And if we are to trust Him completely, we must acknowledge that even when our own vision is cloudy, His vision is perfect. So the next time you're confronted with a challenge that seems too big for you, turn it over to God. No problem is too big for Him...not even yours.

MORE THOUGHTS ABOUT PROBLEMS

Human problems are never greater than divine solutions.

ERWIN LUTZER

Every misfortune, every failure, every loss may be transformed. God has the power to transform all misfortunes into "God-sends."

LETTIE COWMAN

Each problem is a God-appointed instructor.

CHARLES SWINDOLL

Faith points us beyond our problems
to the hope we have in Christ.

BILLY GRAHAM

Everyone gets discouraged. The question is:
Are you going to give up or get up? It's a choice.

JOHN MAXWELL

74

If you make a promise to God, don't be slow to keep it.
God is not happy with fools, so give God what you promised.

ECCLESIASTES 5:4 NCV

OVERCOMING PROCRASTINATION

It's easy—and tempting—to put the tough jobs off until tomorrow. And it's tempting to leave important tasks undone while focusing on busywork. But if we want to be productive human beings, we must learn to do first things first, even when it's hard.

If you find yourself bound by the chains of procrastination, ask yourself what you're waiting for—or more accurately what you're afraid of—and why. As you examine the emotional roadblocks that have, heretofore, blocked your path, you may discover that you're waiting for the "perfect" moment, that instant in time when you feel neither afraid nor anxious. But in truth, perfect moments like these are few and far between.

So stop waiting for the perfect moment and focus, instead, on finding the right moment to do what needs to be done. Then trust God and get busy. When you do, you'll discover that you and the Father, working together, can accomplish great things...and that you can accomplish them sooner rather than later.

Once you acquire the habit of doing what needs to be done when it needs to be done, you will avoid untold trouble, worry, and stress. So learn to overcome procrastination by paying less attention to your fears and more attention to your responsibilities. God has created a world that punishes procrastinators and rewards people who "do it now." In other words, life doesn't procrastinate. Neither should you.

MORE THOUGHTS ABOUT PROCRASTINATION

Our grand business is not to see what lies dimly
at a distance, but to do what lies closely at hand.

THOMAS CARLYLE

God has promised forgiveness to your repentance,
but He has not promised tomorrow to your procrastination.

ST. AUGUSTINE

Don't wait for the "perfect" time to solve your problems.
The "perfect" time to solve them is now.

MARIE T. FREEMAN

The great paralysis of our heart is unbelief.

OSWALD CHAMBERS

75

You will show me the path of life; in Your presence is fullness of joy; at Your right hand are pleasures forevermore.

PSALM 16:11 NKJV

HE WILL SHOW YOU THE PATH

God doesn't do things by accident. He didn't put you here by chance. The Lord didn't deliver you to your particular place, at this particular time, with your particular set of talents and opportunities on a whim. He has a plan, a one-of-a-kind mission designed especially for you. Discovering that plan may take time. But if you keep asking God for guidance, He'll lead you along a path of His choosing and give you every tool you need to fulfill His will.

Of course, you'll probably encounter a few impediments as you attempt to discover the exact nature of God's purpose for your life. And you may travel down a few dead ends along the way. But if you keep searching, and if you genuinely seek the Lord's guidance, He'll reveal His plans at a time and place of His own choosing.

Today and every day, God is beckoning you to hear His voice and follow His plan for your life. When you listen—

and when you answer His call—you'll be amazed at the wonderful things that an all-knowing, all-powerful God can do.

MORE THOUGHTS ABOUT PURPOSE

The easiest way to discover the purpose
of an invention is to ask the creator of it. The same is true
for discovering your life's purpose: Ask God.

RICK WARREN

You weren't an accident. You weren't mass produced.
You aren't an assembly-line product. You were deliberately
planned, specifically gifted, and lovingly positioned
on the Earth by the Master Craftsman.

MAX LUCADO

There's some task which the God of all the universe,
the great Creator has for you to do, and which will
remain undone and incomplete, until by faith
and obedience, you step into the will of God.

ALAN REDPATH

All of God's people are ordinary people who have been
made extraordinary by the purpose he has given them.

OSWALD CHAMBERS

76

Be still, and know that I am God.

PSALM 46:10 KJV

BE STILL

Jesus understood the importance of silence. He spent precious hours alone with God, and so should we. But with our busy schedules, we're tempted to rush from place to place, checking smart phones along the way, leaving no time to contemplate spiritual matters.

You live in a noisy world, a complicated society where sights and sounds surround you and silence is in short supply. Everywhere you turn, or so it seems, the media seeks to grab your attention and hijack your thoughts. You're surrounded by big screens and little ones. And your phone can keep you logged in day and night if you let it. Don't let it.

Today and every day, you need quiet, uninterrupted time alone with God. You need to be still and listen for His voice. And you need to seek His guidance in matters great and small. Your Creator has important plans for your day and your life. And He's trying to get His message through. You owe it to Him—and to yourself—to listen and to learn in silence.

MORE THOUGHTS ABOUT QUIET TIME

Strength is found not in busyness
and noise but in quietness.

LETTIE COWMAN

God's voice is still and quiet and easily buried
under an avalanche of clamor.

CHARLES STANLEY

Nothing in all creation is so like God as stillness.

GOETHE

The world is full of noise. Might we not set ourselves
to learn silence, stillness, solitude?

ELISABETH ELLIOT

I don't see how any Christian can survive,
let alone live life as more than a conqueror,
apart from a quiet time alone with God.

KAY ARTHUR

77

But those who wait on the LORD shall renew their strength;
they shall mount up with wings like eagles,
they shall run and not be weary, they shall walk and not faint.

ISAIAH 40:31 NKJV

TIME FOR RENEWAL

For busy citizens of the twenty-first century, it's easy to become overcommitted, overworked, and over stressed. If we choose, we can be connected 24-7, sparing just enough time for a few hours' sleep each night. What we need is time to renew and recharge, but where can we find the time? We can—and should—find it with God.

God can renew your strength and restore your spirits if you let Him. But He won't force you to slow down, and He won't insist that you get enough sleep at night. He leaves those choices up to you.

If you're feeling chronically tired or discouraged, it's time to rearrange your schedule, turn off the TV, power down the phone, and spend quiet time with your Creator. He knows what you need, and He wants you to experience His peace and His love. He's ready, willing, and perfectly able to renew your strength and help you prioritize the items on your do-list if you ask Him. In fact, He's ready to hear your prayers right now. Please don't make Him wait.

MORE THOUGHTS ABOUT RENEWAL

God specializes in giving people a fresh start.

RICK WARREN

God is not running an antique shop!
He is making all things new!

VANCE HAVNER

The creation of a new heart, the renewing of a right spirit
is an omnipotent work of God. Leave it to the Creator.

HENRY DRUMMOND

Are you weak? Weary? Confused? Troubled? Pressured?
How is your relationship with God? Is it held in its place
of priority? I believe the greater the pressure,
the greater your need for time alone with Him.

KAY ARTHUR

Our Lord never drew power from Himself;
He drew it always from His Father.

OSWALD CHAMBERS

Come unto me, all ye that labor and are heavy laden, and I will give you rest.

MATTHEW 11:28 KJV

ARE YOU GETTING ENOUGH REST?

You inhabit an interconnected world that never slows down and never shuts off. The world tempts you to stay up late watching the news or surfing the Internet or checking out social media or gaming or doing countless other activities that gobble up your time and distract you from more important tasks. But too much late-night screen time robs you of something you need very badly: sleep.

Are you going to bed at a reasonable hour and sleeping through the night? If so, you're both wise and blessed. But if you're staying up late with your eyes glued to a screen, you're putting your long-term health at risk. And you're probably wasting time, too.

So the next time you're tempted to engage in late-night time wasting, resist the temptation. Instead, turn your thoughts and prayers to God. And when you're finished, turn off the lights and go to bed. You need rest more than you need entertainment.

MORE THOUGHTS ABOUT REST

Life is strenuous. See that your clock does not run down.

LETTIE COWMAN

Prescription for a happier and healthier life:
resolve to slow your pace; learn to say no gracefully;
reject the temptation to chase after more pleasures,
more hobbies, and more social entanglements.

JAMES DOBSON

The more comfortable we are with mystery in our journey,
the more rest we will know along the way.

JOHN ELDREDGE

He who cannot rest, cannot work;
he who cannot let go, cannot hold on;
he who cannot find footing, cannot go forward.

HARRY EMERSON FOSDICK

You live among people who glorify busyness.
They've made time a tyrant that controls their lives.

SARAH YOUNG

79

Blessed are those who hunger and thirst for righteousness,
for they will be filled.

MATTHEW 5:6 NIV

THE REWARDS OF RIGHTEOUSNESS

Each day, you make countless decisions that will bring you closer to God, or not. The Lord wants you to live a holy life, a life that reflects an understanding of His Word and a love for His Son.

If we seek God's peace and His blessings, we must respect His teachings and obey them. When we're faced with a difficult choice or a powerful temptation, we should seek God's counsel and trust the counsel He gives.

The Holy Bible contains careful instructions which, if followed, lead to fulfillment and salvation. But if we choose to ignore God's commandments, the results are as predictable as they are tragic. So if you'd like a simple, surefire formula for abundant living, here it is: Live righteously. And for further instructions, read the manual.

MORE THOUGHTS ABOUT RIGHTEOUSNESS

We have two natures within us,
both struggling for mastery. Which one will dominate us?
It depends on which one we feed.

BILLY GRAHAM

You can only learn what obedience is by obeying.

DIETRICH BONHOEFFER

Virtue, even attempted virtue, brings light;
indulgence brings fog.

C. S. LEWIS

Let us never suppose that obedience is impossible
or that holiness is meant only for a select few.
Our Shepherd leads us in paths of righteousness—
not for our name's sake but for His.

ELISABETH ELLIOT

Never support an experience which does not have
God as its source and faith in God as its result.

OSWALD CHAMBERS

Six days shall work be done, but the seventh day is a Sabbath
of solemn rest, a holy convocation. You shall do no work on it;
it is the Sabbath of the LORD in all your dwellings.

LEVITICUS 23:3 NKJV

KEEPING THE SABBATH

Our Father in heaven intends for us to make the Sabbath a
holy day, a day for worship, for contemplation, for fellowship,
and for rest. Yet we live in a seven-day-a-week world, a world
that all too often treats Sunday as a regular workday.

One way to strengthen your faith is by giving God at least
one day each week. If you carve out the time for a day of worship
and praise, you'll be amazed at the impact it will have on the rest
of your week. But if you fail to honor God's day, you'll miss out
on a harvest of blessings that is only available one day each week.

How does your family observe the Lord's day? When
church is over, do you treat Sunday like any other day of the
week? If so, it's time to think long and hard about your family's
schedule and your family's priorities. And if you've been treating
Sunday as just another day, it's time to break that habit. When
Sunday rolls around, don't try to fill every spare moment. Take
time to worship and rest. Father's orders.

MORE THOUGHTS ABOUT THE SABBATH

Jesus spoke about the ox in the ditch on the Sabbath.
But if your ox gets in the ditch every Sabbath,
you should either get rid of the ox or fill up the ditch.

BILLY GRAHAM

God has promised to give you all of eternity.
The least you can do is give Him one day a week in return.

MARIE T. FREEMAN

Where the sabbath is neglected,
religious sensibility goes to decay.

MATTHEW HENRY

You show me a nation that has given up the sabbath,
and I will show you a nation that has got the seed of decay.

D. L. MOODY

Learn to shut out the distractions
that keep you from truly worshipping God.

BILLY GRAHAM

81

Seek the LORD, and his strength: seek his face evermore.
Remember his marvelous works.

PSALM 105:4–5 KJV

SEEK THE LORD

Sometimes, in the crush of our daily duties, God may seem far away, but He is not. God is everywhere we have ever been and everywhere we will ever go. He is with us night and day; He knows our thoughts and our prayers. And when we earnestly seek Him, we will find Him because He is here, waiting patiently for us to reach out to Him.

Today and every day, seek the Lord and lean upon His promises. Trust His Son. Remember that God is always near and that He is your protector and your deliverer. And please remember that no matter your circumstances, God will never leave you. He is always present, always loving, always ready to comfort and protect.

MORE THOUGHTS ABOUT SEEKING GOD

Seeking God first will always put us in
the correct position and aim us in the right direction
to move into the future God has for us.

STORMIE OMARTIAN

The wind of God is always blowing.
But you must hoist your sail.

FRANÇOIS FÈNELON

Lord, who art always the same,
let me know myself, let me know Thee.

ST. AUGUSTINE

Relying on God has to begin all over again
every day as if nothing had yet been done.

C. S. LEWIS

Finding God is really letting God find us; for our search
for him is simply surrender to his search for us.

HARRY EMERSON FOSDICK

82

Be sober, be vigilant; because your adversary the devil walks about like a roaring lion, seeking whom he may devour.

1 PETER 5:8 NKJV

YOUR ADVERSARY IS NEAR

This world can be a dangerous place; enticements are everywhere. Even if you think you're in a very safe place today, be careful. Whether you realize it or not, your adversary is near, waiting for an opening, ready to strike you down if you drop your guard. The enemy has no pity, no compassion, no remorse. And because He's far stronger than you, he'll eventually destroy you if you try to fight Him singlehandedly.

You live in a society that is brimming with temptations and distractions. Never before in the entire history of humankind have adults and children alike been offered access to so many spiritual snares. Never before has the devil had so many tools.

So beware. Take a stand against your enemy. And ask for God's protection. Because your adversary never takes a day off ...and neither should you.

MORE THOUGHTS ABOUT SIN

God has laid down spiritual laws which,
if obeyed, bring harmony and fulfillment,
but, if disobeyed, bring discord and disorder.

BILLY GRAHAM

An unrepented sin is a continued sin.

CORRIE TEN BOOM

An exalted view of God brings a clear view
of sin and a realistic view of self.

HENRY BLACKABY

We cannot out-sin God's ability to forgive us.

BETH MOORE

Could it be that the greatest sin is simply not
to love the Lord your God with all your heart,
mind, soul, and strength?

ANNE GRAHAM LOTZ

83

But grow in the grace and knowledge of our Lord and Savior Jesus Christ.
To Him be the glory both now and forever. Amen.

2 PETER 3:18 NKJV

SPIRITUAL GROWTH

As a Christian, you should never stop growing. No matter your age, no matter your circumstances, you have opportunities to learn and opportunities to serve. Wherever you happen to be, God is there, too, and He wants to bless you with an expanding array of spiritual gifts. Your job is to let Him.

The path to spiritual maturity unfolds day by day. Through prayer, through Bible study, through silence, and through humble obedience to God's Word, we can strengthen our relationship with Him. The more we focus on the Father, the more He blesses our lives. The more carefully we listen for His voice, the more He teaches us.

In the quiet moments when we open our hearts to the Lord, the Creator who made us keeps remaking us. He gives us guidance, perspective, courage, and strength. And the appropriate moment to accept these spiritual gifts is always the present one.

MORE THOUGHTS ABOUT
SPIRITUAL GROWTH

Grow, dear friends, but grow, I beseech you,
in God's way, which is the only true way.

HANNAH WHITALL SMITH

The vigor of our spiritual life will
be in exact proportion
to the place held by the Bible in our life and thoughts.

GEORGE MUELLER

God's ultimate goal for your life on earth
is not comfort, but character development.
He wants you to grow up spiritually
and become like Christ.

RICK WARREN

God will help us become the people we are meant to be,
if only we will ask Him.

HANNAH WHITALL SMITH

84

Finally, be strengthened by the Lord and by His vast strength.

Ephesians 6:10 HCSB

HE IS YOUR STRENGTH

When you're weary or worried, where do you turn for strength? The medicine cabinet? The gym? The health food store? The spa? These places may offer a temporary energy boost, but the best place to turn for strength and solace isn't down the hall or at the mall; it's as near as your next breath. The best source of strength is God.

God's love for you never changes, and neither does His support. From the cradle to the grave, He has promised to give you the strength to meet the challenges of life. He has promised to guide you and protect you if you let Him. But He also expects you to do your part.

Today provides yet another opportunity to partake in the strength that only God can provide. You do so by attuning your heart to Him through prayer, obedience, and trust. Life can be challenging, but fear not. Whatever your challenge, God can give you the strength to face it and overcome it. Let Him.

MORE THOUGHTS ABOUT STRENGTH

Faith is a strong power, mastering any difficulty
in the strength of the Lord who made heaven and earth.

Corrie ten Boom

God is in control. He may not take away trials or make
detours for us, but He strengthens us through them.

Billy Graham

The truth is, God's strength is fully revealed
when our strength is depleted.

Liz Curtis Higgs

God will give us the strength and resources we need
to live through any situation in life that He ordains.

Billy Graham

The strength that we claim from God's Word
does not depend on circumstances. Circumstances
will be difficult, but our strength will be sufficient.

Corrie ten Boom

85

Cast your burden on the LORD, And He shall sustain you;
He shall never permit the righteous to be moved.

PSALM 55:22 NKJV

MANAGING STRESS

Here in the twenty-first century, life can be stressful. So how do we best cope with the challenges of everyday life? By turning our days and our lives over to God. But we're tempted to do the opposite.

Even the most devout Christian may, at times, seek to grab the reins of his or her life and proclaim, "I'm in charge!" To do so is foolish, prideful, and stressful.

When we seek to impose our own wills upon the world—or upon other people—we create needless tension and strain. But when we turn our lives and our hearts over to God—when we accept His will instead of seeking vainly to impose our own—we discover the inner peace that can be ours through Him.

Do you feel overwhelmed by the stresses of daily life? Then turn your concerns and your prayers over to the Lord. He knows your needs and will meet those needs in His own way and in His own time if you let Him. Let Him.

MORE THOUGHTS ABOUT STRESS

Life is strenuous. See that your clock does not run down.

LETTIE COWMAN

There are many burned-out people who think
more is always better, who deem it unspiritual to say no.

SARAH YOUNG

Beware of having so much to do that
you really do nothing at all because
you do not wait upon God to do it aright.

C. H. SPURGEON

God specializes in giving people a fresh start.

RICK WARREN

The more comfortable we are with mystery in our journey,
the more rest we will know along the way.

JOHN ELDREDGE

So then, each of us will give an account of himself to God.

ROMANS 14:12 HCSB

TAKE RESPONSIBILITY

God's Word encourages us to take responsibility for our actions, but the world tempts us to do otherwise. The media tries to convince us that we're "victims" of our upbringing, our government, our economic strata, or our circumstances, thus ignoring the countless blessings—and the gift of free will—that God has given each of us.

Who's responsible for your behavior? God's Word says that you are. If you obey His instructions and follow His Son, you'll be blessed in countless ways. But if you ignore the Lord's teachings, you must eventually bear the consequences of those irresponsible decisions.

Today and every day, as you make decisions about the things you'll say and do, remember who's responsible. And if you make a mistake, admit it, learn from it, and move on. The blame game has no winners; don't play.

MORE THOUGHTS ABOUT RESPONSIBILITY

Firmly entrenched within every human being lies a most
deceptive presupposition: that circumstances and other
people are responsible for our own responses in life.

ERWIN LUTZER

Action springs not from thought,
but from a readiness for responsibility.

DIETRICH BONHOEFFER

We talk about circumstances that are
"beyond our control." None of us have control
over our circumstances, but we are responsible
for the way we pilot ourselves
in the midst of things as they are.

OSWALD CHAMBERS

Work is a blessing. God has so arranged
the world that work is necessary, and He gives us
hands and strength to do it. The enjoyment
of leisure would be nothing if we had only leisure.

ELISABETH ELLIOT

Don't bother to give God instructions;
just report for duty.

CORRIE TEN BOOM

So he who had received five talents came and brought five other talents, saying, "Lord, you delivered to me five talents; look, I have gained five more talents besides them." His lord said to him, "Well done, good and faithful servant; you were faithful over a few things, I will make you ruler over many things. Enter into the joy of your lord."

Matthew 25:20-21 NKJV

USING YOUR TALENTS

God gives each of us special talents and opportunities. And He bestows these gifts for a reason: so that we might use them for His glory. But the world tempts us to do otherwise. Here in the twenty-first century, life is filled to the brim with distractions and temptations, each of which has the potential to distance us from the path God intends us to take.

Do you posses financial resources? Share them. Do you have a spiritual gift? Share it. Do you have a personal testimony about the things that Christ has done for you? Tell your story. Do you possess a particular talent? Hone that skill and use it for God's glory.

All your talents, all your opportunities, and all your gifts are on temporary loan from the Creator. Use those gifts while you can because time is short and the needs are great. In every undertaking, make God your partner. Then, just as He promised, God will bless you now and forever.

MORE THOUGHTS ABOUT YOUR TALENTS

You aren't an accident. You were deliberately planned, specifically gifted, and lovingly positioned on this earth by the Master Craftsman.

MAX LUCADO

It is not my ability, but my response to God's ability, that counts.

CORRIE TEN BOOM

If others don't use their gifts, you get cheated, and if you don't use your gifts, they get cheated.

RICK WARREN

God has given you special talents— now it's your turn to give them back to God.

MARIE T. FREEMAN

Our voices, our service, and our abilities are to be employed, primarily, for the glory of God.

BILLY GRAHAM

88

No temptation has overtaken you except such as is common to man;
but God is faithful, who will not allow you to be tempted beyond
what you are able, but with the temptation will also make
the way of escape, that you may be able to bear it.

1 Corinthians 10:13 NKJV

RESISTING TEMPTATION

This world can be a dangerous place; enticements are everywhere. Even if you think you're in a very safe place today, be careful. Whether you realize it or not, your adversary is near, waiting for an opening, ready to strike you down if you drop your guard. The enemy has no pity, no compassion, no remorse. And because He's far stronger than you, he'll eventually destroy you if you try to fight Him singlehandedly.

You live in a society that is brimming with temptations and distractions. Never before in the entire history of humankind have adults and children alike been offered access to so many spiritual snares. Never before has the devil had so many tools.

So beware. Take a stand against your enemy. And ask for God's protection. Because your adversary never takes a day off ...and neither should you.

MORE THOUGHTS ABOUT TEMPTATION

Temptations that have been anticipated,
guarded against, and prayed about have little power
to harm us. Jesus tells us to "keep watching and praying,
that you may not come into temptation."

JOHN MACARTHUR

Every temptation, directly or indirectly,
is the temptation to doubt and distrust God.

JOHN MACARTHUR

The first step on the way to victory
is to recognize the enemy.

CORRIE TEN BOOM

It is not the temptations you have,
but the decision you make about them, that counts.

BILLY GRAHAM

It is easier to stay out of temptation
than to get out of it.

RICK WARREN

*Therefore, everyone who will acknowledge Me before men,
I will also acknowledge him before My Father in heaven.*

MATTHEW 10:32 HCSB

SHARING YOUR TESTIMONY

We live in a world that desperately needs the healing message of Jesus Christ. And every believer, each in his or her own way, bears a personal responsibility for sharing that message.

In his second letter to Timothy, Paul offers a message to believers of every generation when he writes, "God has not given us a spirit of timidity" (1:7 NASB). Paul's meaning is clear: When sharing our testimonies, we, as Christians, must be courageous, forthright, and unashamed.

If you've been transformed by God's only begotten Son, you know how He has touched your heart and changed your life. Now it's your turn to share the Good News with others. And remember: Now is the perfect time to share your testimony because later may quite simply be too late.

MORE THOUGHTS ABOUT YOUR TESTIMONY

What is your story? Be ready to share it
when the Lord gives you the opportunity.

BILLY GRAHAM

How many people have you made homesick for God?

OSWALD CHAMBERS

Heads are won by reasoning,
but hearts are won by witness-bearing.

C. H. SPURGEON

When your heart is ablaze with the love of God,
then you love other people—especially the rip-snorting
sinners—so much that you dare to tell them
about Jesus with no apologies and no fear.

CATHERINE MARSHALL

The enemy's hope for Christians is that we will
either be so ineffective we have no testimony,
or we'll ruin the one we have.

BETH MOORE

Thanks be unto God for his unspeakable gift.

2 Corinthians 9:15 KJV

A THANKFUL HEART

Each of us has much to be thankful for. We all have more blessings than we can count, beginning with the precious gift of life. Every good gift comes from our Father above, and we owe Him our never-ending thanks. But sometimes, when the demands of everyday life press down upon us, we neglect to express our gratitude to the Creator.

God loves us, He cares for us; He has a plan for each of us; and, He has offered us the gift of eternal life through His Son. Considering all the things that the Lord has done, we owe it to Him—and to ourselves—to slow down many times each day and offer our thanks. His grace is everlasting; our thanks should be too.

SURVIVAL SKILL: THANKSGIVING

Fill up the spare moments of your life
with praise and thanksgiving.

SARAH YOUNG

It is only with gratitude that life becomes rich.

DIETRICH BONHOEFFER

Thanksgiving or complaining—these words express
two contrasting attitudes of the souls of God's children.
The soul that gives thanks can find comfort in everything;
the soul that complains can find comfort in nothing.

HANNAH WHITALL SMITH

Thanksgiving will draw our hearts
out to God and keep us engaged with Him.

ANDREW MURRAY

No matter what our circumstance,
we can find a reason to be thankful.

DAVID JEREMIAH

After this manner therefore pray ye: Our Father which art in heaven,
Hallowed be thy name. Thy kingdom come. Thy will be done in earth,
as it is in heaven. Give us this day our daily bread. And forgive us our debts,
as we forgive our debtors. And lead us not into temptation, but deliver us from evil:
For thine is the kingdom, and the power, and the glory, for ever. Amen

MATTHEW 6:9-13 KJV

MAKING THE LORD'S PRAYER YOUR PRAYER

"Our Father which art in heaven, hallowed be thy name." These familiar words begin the Lord's Prayer, a prayer that you've heard on countless occasions. It's the prayer that Jesus taught his followers to pray, and it's a prayer that you may know by heart.

You already know what the prayer says, but have you thought carefully, and in detail, about exactly what those words mean? Hopefully so.

Today, take the time to carefully consider each word in this beautiful passage. When you weave the Lord's Prayer into the fabric of your life, you'll soon discover that God's Word and God's Son have the power to change everything, including you.

MORE THOUGHTS ABOUT GOD'S WILL

Each and every decision you make,
regardless of its level of intensity,
is vitally important as you seek to do God's will.

ELIZABETH GEORGE

To know the will of God is the highest of all wisdom.

BILLY GRAHAM

The center of God's will is our only safety.

BETSIE TEN BOOM

It is possible to see God's will
in every circumstance and to accept it
with singing instead of complaining.

LETTIE COWMAN

Life's trials are not easy.
But in God's will, each has a purpose.
Often He uses them to enlarge you.

WARREN WIERSBE

Be careful what you think, because your thoughts run your life.

PROVERBS 4:23 NCV

WATCH YOUR THOUGHTS

Because we are human, we are always busy with our thoughts. We simply can't help ourselves. Our brains never shut off, and even while we're sleeping, we mull things over in our minds. The question is not if we will think; the question is how we will think and what we will think about.

Paul Valéry observed, "We hope vaguely but dread precisely." How true. All too often, we allow the worries of everyday life to overwhelm our thoughts and cloud our vision. What's needed is clearer perspective, renewed faith, and a different focus.

When we focus on the frustrations of today or the uncertainties of tomorrow, we rob ourselves of peace in the present moment. But when we direct our thoughts in more positive directions, we rob our worries of the power to tyrannize us.

The American poet Phoebe Cary observed, "All the great blessings of my life are present in my thoughts today." And her words apply to you. You will make your life better when you focus your thoughts on your blessings, not your misfortunes. So do yourself, your family, your friends, and your coworkers a favor: Learn to think optimistically about the world you live in and the life you lead. Then prepare yourself for the blessings that good thoughts will bring.

SURVIVAL SKILL: CLEAR THINKING

It is the thoughts and intents of the heart
that shape a person's life.

JOHN ELDREDGE

Change always starts in your mind.
The way you think determines the way you feel,
and the way you feel influences the way you act.

RICK WARREN

The things we think are the things that feed our souls.
If we think on pure and lovely things, we shall grow pure
and lovely like them; and the converse is equally true.

HANNAH WHITALL SMITH

When you think on the powerful truths of Scripture,
God uses His Word to change your way of thinking.

ELIZABETH GEORGE

Your life today is a result of your thinking yesterday.
Your life tomorrow will be determined by what you think today.

JOHN MAXWELL

93

*Teach us to number our days carefully
so that we may develop wisdom in our hearts.*

PSALM 90:12 HCSB

MANAGING TIME

Time is a nonrenewable gift from the Lord. But sometimes we treat our time here on earth as if it were not a gift at all: We're tempted to invest our lives in trivial pursuits, pointless pastimes, and petty diversions. But our Father beckons each of us to a higher calling.

An important element of our stewardship to God is the way that we choose to spend the time He has entrusted to us. Each waking moment holds the potential to do a good deed, to say a kind word, or to offer a heartfelt prayer. Our challenge, as believers, is to use our time wisely in the service of God's children and in accordance with His plan for our lives.

Each day is a special treasure to be savored and celebrated. May we—as Christians who have so much to celebrate—never fail to praise our Creator by rejoicing in this glorious day, and by using it wisely.

MORE THOUGHTS ABOUT MANAGING TIME

Energy and time are limited entities.
Therefore, we need to use them wisely,
focusing on what is truly important.

SARAH YOUNG

Life is short; none of us knows how long we have.
Live each day as if it were your last—
for someday it will be.

BILLY GRAHAM

Time is your most precious gift,
because you only have a set amount of it.

RICK WARREN

The choices of time are binding in eternity.

JACK MACARTHUR

We are accountable to God
for the way we use our time.

BILLY GRAHAM

This is the day the LORD has made; we will rejoice and be glad in it.

PSALM 118:24 NKJV

THIS IS THE DAY

All the days on the calendar have one thing in common: They're all gifts from God. So this day, like every day, is a cause for celebration as we consider God's blessings and His love.

How will you invest this day? Will you treat your time as a commodity too precious to be squandered? Will you carve out time during the day to serve God by serving His children? Will you celebrate God's gifts and obey His commandments? And will you share words of encouragement with the people who cross your path? The answers to these questions will determine, to a surprising extent, the quality of your day and the quality of your life.

So, wherever you find yourself today, take time to celebrate and give thanks for another priceless gift from the Father. The present moment is precious. Treat it that way.

MORE THOUGHTS ABOUT TODAY

Yesterday is the tomb of time,
and tomorrow is the womb of time.
Only now is yours.

R. G. LEE

The one word in the spiritual vocabulary is now.

OSWALD CHAMBERS

Today is mine. Tomorrow is none of my business.
If I peer anxiously into the fog of the future,
I will strain my spiritual eyes so that I will not
see clearly what is required of me now.

ELISABETH ELLIOT

Each day is God's gift of a fresh unspoiled opportunity
to live according to His priorities.

ELIZABETH GEORGE

Faith does not concern itself with the entire journey.
One step is enough.

LETTIE COWMAN

Trust in the LORD with all your heart, and lean not on your own understanding;
In all your ways acknowledge Him, and He shall direct your paths.

PROVERBS 3:5-6 NKJV

TRUST HIM

As we pass through this world, we travel past peaks and valleys. When we reach the mountaintops of life, we find it easy to praise God and to give thanks. And as we reach the crest of the mountain's peak, we find it easy to trust God's plan. But when we find ourselves in the dark valleys of life, when we face disappointment, despair, or heartbreak, it's much more difficult to trust God. Yet, trust Him we must.

As Christians, we can be comforted: Whether we find ourselves at the pinnacle of the mountain or the darkest depths of the valley, God is there. And we Christians have every reason to live courageously. After all, Christ has already won the ultimate battle on the cross at Calvary.

So the next time you find your courage tested to the limit, lean upon God's promises. Trust His Son. Remember that God is always near and that He is your protector and your deliverer. When you are worried, anxious, or afraid, call upon Him. God can handle your problems infinitely better than you can, so turn them over to Him. Remember that God rules both mountaintops and valleys—with limitless wisdom and love—now and forever.

SURVIVAL SKILL: TRUSTING GOD

One of the marks of spiritual maturity is the quiet confidence that God is in control, without the need to understand why he does what he does.

CHARLES SWINDOLL

Never yield to gloomy anticipation. Place your hope and confidence in God. He has no record of failure.

LETTIE COWMAN

Faith and obedience are bound up in the same bundle. He that obeys God, trusts God; and he that trusts God, obeys God.

C. H. SPURGEON

When a train goes through a tunnel and it gets dark, you don't throw away your ticket and jump off. You sit still and trust the engineer.

CORRIE TEN BOOM

YOUR EMERGENCY VERSE ABOUT WISDOM

Get wisdom—how much better it is than gold!
And get understanding—it is preferable to silver.

PROVERBS 16:16 HCSB

ACQUIRING WISDOM

God's Word makes this promise: If we genuinely desire wisdom, and if we're willing to search for it, we will find it. And where should the search begin? The answer, of course, is in God's Holy Word.

The search for wisdom should be a lifelong journey, not a destination. We should continue to read, to watch, and to learn new things as long as we live. But it's not enough to learn new things or to memorize the great Biblical truths; we must also live by them.

So what will you learn today? Will you take time to feed your mind and fill your heart? And will you study the guidebook that God has given you? Hopefully so, because His plans and His promises are waiting for you there, inside the covers of a book like no other: His Book. It contains the essential wisdom you'll need to navigate the seas of life and land safely on that distant shore.

SURVIVAL SKILL: WISDOM

Wisdom is the right use of knowledge. To know is not
to be wise. There is no fool so great as the knowing fool.
But, to know how to use knowledge is to have wisdom.

C. H. Spurgeon

Knowledge is horizontal. Wisdom is vertical;
it comes down from above.

Billy Graham

True wisdom is marked by willingness to listen
and a sense of knowing when to yield.

Elizabeth George

Wisdom is the power to see and the inclination
to choose the best and highest goal,
together with the surest means of attaining it.

J. I. Packer

Knowledge can be found in books or in school.
Wisdom, on the other hand, starts with God...and ends there.

Marie T. Freeman

97

And whatever you do, do it heartily, as to the Lord and not to men.

Colossians 3:23 NKJV

DO THE WORK

The old saying is both familiar and true: We should pray as if everything depended upon the Lord but work as if everything depended upon us. Yet sometimes, when we are tired or discouraged, our worries can sap our strength and sidetrack our motivation. But God has other intentions. He expects us to work for the things that we pray for. More importantly, God intends that our work should become His work.

As you seek to accomplish your goals and fulfill God's plan for your life, your success will depend, in large part, upon the passion that you bring to your work. God has created a world in which hard work is rewarded and laziness is not. So don't look for shortcuts (because there aren't any) and don't expect easy solutions to life's biggest challenges (because big rewards usually require lots of effort). You inhabit a world in which instant gratification is rare, but the rewards of hard work are not. Shape your expectations—and your work habits—accordingly.

MORE THOUGHTS ABOUT WORK

God did not intend for us to be idle and unproductive.
There is dignity in work.

BILLY GRAHAM

When love and skill work together,
expect a masterpiece.

JOHN RUSKIN

Pray as though everything depended on God.
Work as though everything depended on you.

ST. AUGUSTINE

Ordinary work, which is what most of us do
most of the time, is ordained by God
every bit as much as is the extraordinary.

ELISABETH ELLIOT

It may be that the day of judgment will dawn tomorrow;
in that case, we shall gladly stop working for a better future.
But not before.

DIETRICH BONHOEFFER

98

Do not love the world or the things in the world.
If anyone loves the world, the love of the Father is not in him.

1 John 2:15 NKJV

IN THE WORLD, BUT NOT OF THE WORLD

We live in this world, but we should not worship it. Yet, we are bombarded by messages and distractions that tempt us to do otherwise. The twenty-first-century world in which we live is a noisy, confusing place. The world seems to cry, "Worship me with your money, your time, your energy, your thoughts, and your life." But if we are wise, we won't worship the world; we will worship God.

If you wish to build your character day by day, you must distance yourself, at least in part, from the temptations and distractions of modern-day society. But distancing yourself isn't easy, especially when so many societal forces are struggling to capture your attention, your participation, and your money.

All of mankind is engaged in a colossal, worldwide treasure hunt. Some people seek treasure from earthly sources; others seek God's treasures by making Him the cornerstone of their lives. What kind of treasure hunter are you? Are you so caught up in the demands of everyday living that you sometimes allow the search for worldly treasures to become your primary focus? If so, it's time to reorganize your daily to-do list by placing God in His rightful place: first place. Don't allow anyone or anything to separate you from your heavenly Father and His only begotten Son.

MORE THOUGHTS ABOUT WORLDLINESS

The voices of the world are a cacophony of chaos,
pulling you this way and that. Don't listen to those voices.

SARAH YOUNG

We live in a hostile world that constantly seeks
to pull us away from God.

BILLY GRAHAM

Loving the world destroys our relationship
with God, it denies our faith in God,
and it discounts our future with God.

DAVID JEREMIAH

We need more love for the word
and less love for the world.

R. G. LEE

But seek first the kingdom of God and His righteousness, and all these things shall be added to you. Therefore do not worry about tomorrow, for tomorrow will worry about its own things. Sufficient for the day is its own trouble.

MATTHEW 6:33-34 NKJV

ABOVE AND BEYOND WORRY

Because we are fallible human beings struggling through the inevitable challenges of life here on earth, we worry. Even though we, as Christians, have been promised the gift of eternal life—even though we, as Christians, are blessed by God's love and protection—we find ourselves fretting over the inevitable frustrations of everyday life.

Where is the best place to take your worries? Take them to God. Take your concerns to Him; take your fears to Him; take your doubts to Him; take your weaknesses to Him; take your sorrows to Him...and leave them all there. Seek protection from the Creator and build your spiritual house upon the Rock that cannot be moved. Remind yourself that God still sits in His heaven and you are His beloved child. Then, perhaps, you will worry less and trust Him more. And that's as it should be because the Lord is trustworthy...and you are protected.

MORE THOUGHTS ABOUT WORRY

Worry and anxiety are sand in the machinery of life;
faith is the oil.

E. Stanley Jones

Look around you and you'll be distressed;
look within yourself and you'll be depressed;
look at Jesus, and you'll be at rest!

Corrie ten Boom

Do not hide from your fear or pretend
that it isn't there. Anxiety that you hide in the recesses
of your heart will give birth to fear of fear.

Sarah Young

The beginning of anxiety is the end of faith,
and the beginning of true faith is the end of anxiety.

George Mueller

Never yield to gloomy anticipation. Place your hope
and confidence in God. He has no record of failure.

Lettie Cowman

100

I was glad when they said unto me, Let us go into the house of the LORD.

PSALM 122:1 KJV

WORSHIP HIM SEVEN DAYS A WEEK

To worship God is a privilege, but it's a privilege that far too many of us forego. Instead of praising our Creator seven days a week, we worship on Sunday mornings (if at all) and spend the rest of the week focusing on other things.

Whenever we become distracted by worldly pursuits that put God in second place, we inevitably pay the price of our misplaced priorities. A better strategy, of course, is to worship Him every day of the week, beginning with a regular early-morning devotional.

Every new day provides another opportunity to worship God with grateful hearts and helping hands. And each day offers another chance to support the church He created. When we do so, we bless others—and we are blessed by the One who sent His only begotten Son so that we might have eternal life.

SURVIVAL SKILL: WORSHIP

Worship is an inward reverence,
the bowing down of the soul in the presence of God.

ELIZABETH GEORGE

Even the most routine part of your day
can be a spiritual act of worship.

SARAH YOUNG

Worship in the truest sense takes place
only when our full attention is on God—His glory,
majesty, love, and compassion.

BILLY GRAHAM

Worship is focus.

BETH MOORE

We must worship in truth.
Worship is not just an emotional exercise
but a response of the heart built on truth about God.

ERWIN LUTZER

DaySpring

LIVE YOUR FAITH

Dear Friend,

This book was prayerfully crafted with you, the reader, in mind—every word, every sentence, every page—was thoughtfully written, designed, and packaged to encourage you...right where you are this very moment. At DaySpring, our vision is to see every person experience the life-changing message of God's love. So, as we worked through rough drafts, design changes, edits and details, we prayed for you to deeply experience His unfailing love, indescribable peace, and pure joy. It is our sincere hope that through these Truth-filled pages your heart will be blessed, knowing that God cares about you—your desires and disappointments, your challenges and dreams.

He knows. He cares. He loves you unconditionally.

BLESSINGS!
THE DAYSPRING BOOK TEAM

Additional copies of this book and
other DaySpring titles can be purchased
at fine bookstores everywhere.
Order online at dayspring.com
or
by phone at 1-877-751-4347